THE CREATION OF WOMAN

MICHELANGELO: *The Creation of Eve.* Sistine Chapel

THE CREATION
OF WOMAN

by THEODOR REIK

George Braziller, Inc.
New York — 1960

TO MY DAUGHTER THEODORA

CONTENTS

"And God said, Let us make man in our image, after our likeness: and let them have dominion over the fish of the sea, and over the fowl of the air, and over the cattle, and over all the earth, and over every creeping thing that creepeth upon the earth.

"So God created man in his own image, in the image of God created he him; male and female created he them."

Genesis, I, 26, 27

"And the Lord God formed man of the dust of the ground, and breathed into his nostrils the breath of life; and man became a living soul. . . .

And the Lord God caused a deep sleep to fall upon Adam, and he slept: and he took one of his ribs, and closed up the flesh instead thereof;

And the rib, which the Lord God had taken from man, made he a woman, and brought her unto the man.

And Adam said, This is now bone of my bones, and flesh of my flesh: she shall be called Woman, because she was taken out of Man.

Therefore shall a man leave his father and his mother, and shall cleave unto his wife: and they shall be one flesh. . . ."

Genesis, II, 7, 21-24

Introduction

IF IT were possible to transplant a moment of the past into the present, a few moments from a court scene (which the New York *Times* called the most amazing in Anglo-Saxon history) would be the best introduction for this book. The scene is the little town of Dayton, Tennessee, on one of the hottest days of July 1925.[1] The numerous visitors to Dayton are greeted by banners which say: "Read your Bible daily!" and "Where will you spend eternity?" and "Sweethearts, come to Jesus!" It is the fourth day of the trial of John T. Scopes who dared to teach the theory of evolution in a school in Tennessee. The examination of the witnesses takes place in the yard outside the courtroom. Here, in the torrid heat, William Jennings Bryan, untiring preacher of fundamentalism, takes the stand as an expert on the Bible. Coatless, his sleeves rolled up, he fans himself with a palm leaf. The attorney for the defense, Clarence Darrow, who has called him to the stand to testify, is also in his shirtsleeves. He asks:

"Mr. Bryan, do you believe that the first woman was Eve?"
Answer: "Yes."
Question: "Do you believe she was literally made out of Adam's rib?"
Answer: "I do."
During those days Darrow asked his friend, Arthur Garfield Hayes, who had joined him in defending the teacher Scopes: "Isn't it difficult to realize that a trial of this kind is possible in

11

the twentieth century in the United States?" Actually, it is not difficult to imagine a similar trial today, only thirty-four years later, in this, our age of conformity, religious revival and bigotry.

This book, however, is not concerned with those contemporary problems. To call up the memory of that court scene from the recent past should serve only to raise the curtain on a performance that will take us back to the beginning of time, to the dawn of creation. Written without scholarly pretentions, this essay takes as its point of departure the myth—if myth is the appropriate word—of the creation of woman, the same myth which was a subject of testimony in that famous, or infamous, Scopes trial. We will, therefore, start from that Biblical narrative—from a few sentences of the second chapter of Genesis. But neither textual investigation nor higher criticism is our aim. Those few verses (Gen. II: 21-24) will be treated here in a manner similar to that of the archeologist who deciphers a puzzling ancient inscription.

Freud once remarked[2] that the Biblical story of Eve's creation has "something about it that is quite peculiar and singular." I am convinced that the hidden meaning of that Biblical account has not yet been discovered. The Genesis report of the creation of woman is still as bristling with mysteries as a porcupine with quills. Our first task will be the reconstruction of the primal tradition from which the Biblical narrative, often altered and distorted, evolved. New clues, emerging from an unexpected source, led me to a hidden path. The analytic exploration of this primeval hiding place enabled me to uncover the unknown original tradition of the myth. Its reconstruction provides us with new insights which could not have been reached in any other way. The discovery of the original meaning of the creation myth will serve, then, as a kind of peephole through which we may look into secret realms of prehistory. It is to be hoped that future research in the field of the ancient Near East and in comparative religion will excavate many hidden treasures of knowledge whose location is first pointed to in the attempt undertaken here.

This book belongs to the realm of archeological psycho-analysis. I gave this name to a still undeveloped branch of psychoanalytic research which explores problems of prehistory.[3] It does so by applying the combined methods of comparative history and anthropology with the analytic observation and evaluation of details until now neglected. Following the great tradition of my master and friend, Sigmund Freud, I have shown in various books and papers that such problems which have been tackled in vain by other methods of research can be brought closer to solution with the help of the new tools which psycho-analysis provides. If I am not mistaken, the present adventure in psychoanalytic discovery will cast a new light not only on the earliest traditions of the Bible, but also on the origin of its people.

THEODOR REIK

New York, October 1959.

PART ONE

THE MYTH
AND THE MYSTERY
OF EVE

CHAPTER I

THE TWO STORIES

THE CREATION of man is a theme central to the myths of most primitive peoples and ancient civilizations. Yet it was at first no enigma. It became one only after a certain degree of self-awareness was reached, when man conceived of himself as a separate part of nature. Even then, the wish to know was not urgent, and curiosity about the origin of man was only casually expressed and easily satisfied. To a native of southern Australia it was sufficient to learn that Bunjil, the eagle hawk, made man and things. The Bushman was content with the information that Cagn, identified with the mantis insect, was the creator. Among the native tribes of America, the coyote, the crow, the raven or the hare played the chief role in the creation of man.

The first myths are, it seems to me, produced by, and meant for, men. They often become, it is true, old wives' tales, but only long after they have been contemptuously dismissed by the men of the tribe. Women are more often occupied than preoccupied with the creation of man. Their imagination is not involved with the solution to the question of how the first human being was created. This is no problem for them: they know. It could not have been very different, they feel, from the manner in which their own children are born. The myths and legends of creation, including those of the Bible, presuppose an audience of men.

As long ago as 1683, C. Vitringa recognized a dual account of the creation of man in the opening chapters of Genesis. He

recognized that the first and the second chapters present a striking discrepancy. In the first chapter the Lord is depicted as
creating all living beings in the water and in the air, and forming all terrestial animals. Then, last of all, on the sixth day He
created man. Fashioned in God's own image, man is the zenith
of creation. Man and woman were produced simultaneously
("male and female created He them.") When we turn to the
second chapter, quite a different picture is presented: in contrast to and in contradiction with that first account we learn
that God created man initially, then the lower animals and last
of all—almost as an afterthought—woman, whom he fashioned
from Adam's rib.

The differences in order and content are obvious. The chro-
nology in the two accounts is reversed. In the second narrative,
mention is made of man having been created in the image of
his Creator. He is formed of the dust of the ground and God
breathed into his nostrils the breath of life. Only then did man
become a living soul. In the first version the Lord appears as a
creator; in the second as a molder and mover of man.

Biblical commentators add to these differences several others:
in the first version God is called *Elohim*, while the second version employs a combination of *Yahweh* and *Elohim*. Furthermore, palpable dissimilarities in style occur. The one account,
from the first chapter to the third verse of the second, the critics
assert,[1] is systematic and stereotyped, verbose and chronological. In the second chapter there is a complete change in style:
it is free, poetical and picturesque.

Bible critics traced these discrepancies back to the fact that
the two accounts are derived from two separate main sources: an
older one belonging to the Yahwist document and a later
narrative written for the Priestly report. It should be mentioned
en passant that the Yahwist story itself is by no means uniform.
Several contradictions and anomalies are contained in it: the
Paradise is, according to II:8, situated in the far East; according
to II:20, in the West land, and according to II:16, in the North.

The expulsion from the Garden of Eden is told twice, the curse
upon man is repeated, and so on. The two strands from which
the Yahwist draws are usually differentiated as Jj and Ye.

We shall not enter into the discussion of the definition and
division of the material according to sources. Biblical scholars,
quoting chapter and verse, do not yet agree about them. It is
also beyond the scope of this investigation to trace the individual sources back to mythological patterns of the people of
the ancient Orient. Suffice it to say that the first account was
often compared to the Assyro-Bablyonian cosmogony with
which some striking similarities were discovered. Several attempts
were made to trace the Yahwist narrative of the creation of
man to one or another mythological tale of some ancient
people, but to date no such comparable account has been
found. There is a possibility that we may discover a common
Semitic tradition from which the two cosmogonies were descended.

The German scholar Gerhard von Rade recently compared the
whole biblical account of the creation to a structure based
upon two powerful mythological columns which we call the
Yahwistic and the Priestly. Yet the same scholar has warned
us not to overemphasize the definiteness of the traditions as
they have come down to us.[2] He says that however late one dates
the Yahwist editor, measured by the tradition included in
his narrative, his written report "marks an end for that material which had already had a long history behind it."[3] It is this
old oral tradition much more than the actual Biblical text that
interests us here.

A few remarks on the relation between the two sources from
which the two editors took their material is necessary. Biblical
scholars assume that the Yahwist, or the group of writers to
whom they have given this name, is the older editor. His text
was probably written about 850 B.C. in the Southern Kingdom
of Judah. The Priestly document was written in the sixth century
during the exile. The older narrative is richer in folklore and

offers, as J. G. Frazer remarks, "more points of comparison
with the childlike stories by which man in many ages and
countries have sought to explain the great mystery of the beginning of life on earth." Most scholars concluded from the
age of the Yahwist editor that he has preserved many features
of primitive simplicity which the later Priestly document has
effaced. Yet the fact that the Yahwist has retained those features
does not necessarily mean that the saga material he used is itself
older and more primitive than that of his later colleague.

It is quite possible that the Yahwist (although he comes at
least two hundred and fifty years earlier than the Priestly editor
and is simpler and more primitive in his treatment of sagas)
could have drawn from younger story material than the other,
who dealt with the tradition in a more "modern" manner. We
are inclined to forget that both editors were primarily story-
tellers, and that their chief purpose was the preservation and
transmission of traditions which had lived for many hundreds of
years in the Hebrew tribes and which had been told at camp-
fires and in tents.

The age in which a writer lives and his manner of writing are
not the only factors decisive in determining the period to which
the subject matter belongs. Shakespeare wrote the story of
Richard the Second, who reigned not so long before his time;
and our contemporary poet, Richard Beer-Hofman, wrote a
verse tragedy about King David. In other words, it is conceivable
that the Priestly editor, although he lived so much later, used
older material than did his predecessor. The Yahwist, in dealing
with the same general material—for instance, with the creation
of woman—might have chosen a much more recent version of
the oral tradition of the people for his account in Genesis.

In order to clear the deck, another aspect of the question of
the two main sources must be considered. It immediately brings
us close to our special subject. The discrepancies between the
two Biblical accounts were, of course, noticed very early. The
rabbis of Talmudic times reflected upon them often and tried to

harmonize the contradictory narratives. So did the church fathers and their successors, the Christian theologians. Some commentators of our age have also made desperate, if futile, attempts at reconciliation in this direction. While modern Biblical criticism is content to state the differences of the versions and to trace them back to their origin in the two main sources of tradition, rigid defenders of the unity of the Bible either deny the existence of any disharmonies or casually rationalize and minimize them.

In restricting ourselves to the treatment of our subject, which is the myth of the creation of woman, we shall sketch the main answers that have been given to the questions raised by the two contradictory versions. Folklore itself found an ingenious way of bringing the two accounts into agreement: if, in the one version, God created man as male and female, and, in the other, woman was fashioned from Adam's rib, our earliest ancestor must have been a widower or a "divorced" man when the Lord led Eve to him. Or did Adam have two wives at one time? This might bring the two Biblical narratives into harmony. Some legends tell us that there was another woman in Adam's life before Eve appeared. Her name was Lilith. The figure of Lilith is perhaps originally that of a Babylonian night-demon. Lilith was supposed to have been Adam's first wife, created out of earth just as he was, and together with him. According to the legend this first wife of Adam remained with him only a short time and then left him, because she insisted on enjoying full equality with him. She flew away and vanished into thin air. Adam complained about this to the Lord, saying that his wife had deserted him; the angels then found her in the Red Sea. Lilith, however, refused to return to her husband and lived on as an evil demon who injured newborn babies.[4] This saga, to be found in the Zohar, has been retained by some Jews in the ghettos of the East. Older sources already speak of a "first Eve." In some legends Lilith appears as male and female.

The other way in which the discrepancies between the two

stories of the creation were dealt with was to deny their existence. Rigid defenders of the fundamentalist view put forward
all kinds of sophistic and misleading arguments, based on un-
sound reasoning, but persuasive for the believers. Thus, it has
often been stated that the second chapter of Genesis does not
present a new narrative of the creation, but simply sets forth in
greater detail the story of the creation of man.

It was argued that the scholars who insist on different sources
make an arbitrary assumption and create a contradiction where
none exists. From this point of view, the second chapter is not
a duplicate but a sequel to the first, whose content it duly regards.
The story of the creation is not told again; the intention of the
author was not, as modern critics maintain, to treat the same
subject again and in a different manner. According to this argument the narrator did not invert the chronological order in which
the creation took place nor the amount of time it took; he did
not reduce the number of days from six to one. The first Biblical
chapter describes the creation of the universe in a kind of synthesis of the whole. It advances without interruption "from the
initial inanimate matter to the culmination of the whole grand
process in the creation of man in the image of God."[5] In contrast but not in contradiction to this report, the second chapter
does not discuss the abstract order of creation, says nothing
of the creation of heaven, of the earth and the stars; but starts
with planting the Garden of Eden.

Yet the contradictions between the two creation accounts are
so numerous and flagrant that every attempt to reconcile them
is doomed to fail. If, therefore, the defenders of the traditional
view are undoubtedly mistaken, does this make the opinions of
their adversaries correct? Does the assumption of two different
sources for the Genesis story remove the difficulties? How are we
to explain the preservation, side by side, of two versions with
such amazing dissimilarities? Are those scholars justified who
assert that the author of the second chapter could not have intended to retell the story of creation, which in his account would

be not only sketchy and unsatisfactory, but also contradict the other tradition?

A new interpretation would have to explain not only those inconsistencies and dissimilarities, but would have to clarify and finally resolve the long controversy. It would also have to explain how the divergent accounts were preserved within the Holy Scripture.

The truth about the primal tradition of the creation may not lie between the extreme views of fundamentalists and higher criticism, but beyond them, on a different plane.

CHAPTER II

THE FIRST HUMAN BEING
A MAN-WOMAN?

J. G. FRAZER describes the rudimentary concepts of the origin of mankind common to the Greeks, Hebrews, Egyptians and Babylonians.[1] He does not doubt that those primitive notions were handed down to the civilized people of antiquity by their savage and barbarous forefathers. Similar stories are recorded among the savage tribes of yesterday and today. We shall, perhaps, have occasion to relate some of them and compare them with the Biblical account of the creation of man and woman.

This comparison suggests another train of thought, concerning the universal interest of primitive people in the difference between the sexes. The other day I came across a recent book, whose subject leads us back to the world of the stone-age savages mentioned by Frazer, and which has the characteristic title *Adam with Arrows*.[2] The author, Colin Simpson, describes the life of the savage Kikuyu in New Guinea today and in one passage alludes to this interest. He does not discuss their stories of the creation of man, but reflects upon the feelings the natives must have experienced when the first white people entered into their world. Who can say, for instance, what the first airplane would have looked like to stone-age people? We can only guess. Perhaps one of the writer's friends is right when he thinks that the monstrous, roaring, stiff-winged object might have appeared to them as a "dragon-bird." A crowd of Kikuyu came to the landing strip and brought bags full of food for the airplane. (After all, living things must eat). The most venturesome of the natives got down on their hands and knees and peered underneath the fuselage. A Marobe policeman, grinning with superior knowledge, explained that they were looking for its genitals, to see if the "dragon-bird" was male or female. (You might know a lot about such a monstrous thing if you could find out its sex!)

Returning to our subject, we think of the first chapter of the Scripture that tells us that God created man in His own image: "male and female created He them." Frazer remarks[3] that it seems that the distinction of the sexes is shared by the divinity "though how the distinction can be reconciled with the unity of the Godhead is a point on which the writer vouchsafes us no information." Frazer passes this theological problem by as if it might be too profound for human comprehension.[4] Other scholars considered the difficulty within the realm of human understanding and found easy explanations for it.

Several Biblical commentators pointed out in vain that the word "create" must be understood not metaphorically but realistically.[5] The expression used for the Lord's production method is described by the same word applied in the Old Testament (Isa. XXIX:10; Jer. XVIII:4) for the potter molding clay. It helped those commentators little when they could prove that in different oriental texts of ancient times a god or a goddess is depicted forming man.

Some commentators assert that the Biblical story conceives of Adam as male and female simultaneously. The plural, used in the sentence "created He them," in its purposeful contrast to the previous singular, "created He him," seemed to preclude the assumption of a primal androgynous human being. Yet they argue that the sacred text speaks of creation in God's image and

they ask, with gentle allusion to the passage "man and woman
created He them," how one should imagine that "image" otherwise than male and female simultaneously. They deny that it
is only a grammatical or semantic question posed here. Not
satisfied with the information that all is possible for the Lord,
they take upon themselves the mystery of things as if, to speak
with Lear, we were God's spies. Strangely enough, it was not
the doubters and agnostics, but the religious people who first
showed such irreverent curiosity.

The interpretation that Adam was created as man-woman, as
androgynous, already emerges in rabbinical literature.[6] Eusebius,
the church father, pointed out that this view is related to that
in Plato's *Symposium* (189d,190d) where the myth of the primal
double-sexed being is reported. Alfred Jeremiah has shown that
a similar view is to be found among the Babylonians.[7] In the
philosophical interpretations of Philo of Alexandria, the mythological conception of the first androgynous being is "still dis-
cernible."[8] It is, however, clearly formulated by the Gnostics.

In the legends of the Jews and in Talmudic commentaries
(especially of later periods) the tradition of a primal androgynous
being is preserved. For example, Rabbi Jeremiah ben Eleazar,
said:[9] "Adam was doublefaced, since it is said (Psalm Cxxxix;5)
'Thou hast made me behind and before' ". The one face was
male, the other female. Other rabbis explain that Adam and Eve
were created back to back, joined at their shoulders; then God
separated them by a blow with a hatchet or by sawing them in
half.

In a recent monograph Ernst Benz follows the myth of the
androgynous Adam from the Gnostic writers to the modern
mystics.[10] The philosophical and theological speculations of
Judah Abravanel (about 1460-1525) were followed by the reflections of the German mystic Jacob Boehme (1575-1624) concerning a primal being functioning as man and woman. This
godlike creature described in Boehme's *Mysterium Magnum* has

no eyelashes and needs no sleep. This glorious being was divided
by God into man and woman and was punished after the Fall
by sleep. The circle of Philadelphians around John Pordage
(1607-1681) and the theosophist Emanuel Swedenborg (1689-
1772) renewed speculations of this kind. The French Louis de
Saint Martin (1743-1803) in his *"L'homme de Désir,"* the Rus-
sians Nikolaj Berdidjajew and Wladimir Sokojew (1853-1900),
made the myth of the androgynous primal being the foundation
of their metaphysical systems of love and sex.

One of the most interesting philsophers who conceived Adam
as androgynous was Leone Ebreo, a physician who, because of
the persecution of the Jews in Spain, fled to Naples and there
in 1501-02 wrote his most enduring work, *Dialoghi d'Amore*.[11]
This book consists of three dialogues between Philo, the lover,
and Sophia (wisdom), his beloved, in which Philo, the seeker
after truth, tells his sweetheart the myth of the androgynous
being, as Aristophanes reports it in Plato's *Symposium*. He asserts, however, that the origin of that myth is to be found in the
sacred writings of Moses, concerning the creation of the first
human parents, Adam and Eve. Sophia is astonished and says:
"I never heard that Moses composed that myth." But her friend
explains: "He did not so plainly, nor in such detail, but the
substance of the story he told briefly. It was from him that
Plato took his myth, amplifying and polishing it after the manner of Greek oratory, thus giving a new and confused account of
the Hebrew version.[12]

This concept tracing the Platonic myth back to forgotten Hebrew traditions is to be expected from a religious Jew of Leone
Ebreo's time. It is more astonishing that some modern scholars
still assume that the Biblical story embodied the myth of a male-
female ancestor of mankind. Ernst Benz's aforementioned book
is a case in point; in it he states that the editor of the Adam story
in Genesis knew an old tradition of this kind. This editor reshaped the original saga in such a way that the present account

of the creation of man and woman took the place of the earlier
legend.

Half a century before the speculations of Benz, a serious
scholar like Friedrich Schwally asserted that the Genesis story
originally conceives of Adam as androgynous.[13] Sober critics
like Joseph Feldman considered Schwally's hypothesis entirely
unfounded, *völlig haltlos*.[14] They point out that such tradition
is excluded in advance by the inference that the divinity in
whose image the male-female primal being was created had to
be himself, or herself, androgynous. Rather, Feldman justifiably
adds, one could recognize a contrast to such mythological notions in the Biblical presentation.

But to return to the interpretation of "Master Leon Abrabanel,
the physician," as he was called in Spain, or Leon the Jew, as
he was known elsewhere: more remarkable than his conception
of the androgynous nature of Adam was the fact that Leone
Ebreo very acutely pointed out the contradictions in the creation story. In other words, more than five hundred and sixty
years ago—at the time when Columbus went out to discover a
new world,—this philosopher had already anticipated results of
modern higher criticism. (As a matter of historic fact, Leon's
father, Don Isaac, in the service of Ferdinand and Isabella, as-
sisted in raising money for Columbus' first expedition.)

Philo calls Sophia's attention to the fact that the Genesis
stories are full of contradictions: "For it first says that God
created Adam on the sixth day, both male and female; then
that God said, 'It is not good that the man should be alone'. . . .
and He created Eve as female counterpart of Adam." "The
woman," says Leone, "was, therefore, not made in the beginning
as was first said." At the end of the narrative we read that God
created man in His likeness, male and female, and He called
their name Adam. "It would appear, therefore, that there was
at once both male and female at the beginning of the creation,
and that the woman was not made subsequently by the with-

drawal of the side or rib as is narrated." Leone Ebreo then dem-
onstrates clear contradictions in each of the two texts. God is
said to have created Adam in His own image, male and female
created He them. Yet, the philosopher argues, "Adam is the
name of the first man, and the woman was called Eve when she
was created. God, therefore, in creating Adam and not Eve, only
created a male and not male and female as the text says." Moreover, the words at the end of the narrative are even more
abstruse: "These are the generations of Adam. In the day when
God created him, male and female created He them and called
their name Adam in the day that they were created." Here we
observe that God in creating Adam, made both male and female.
Yet, He called them both by the name Adam in the day that
they were created. No mention is made of Eve, which is the
name of the female part of man, although we have already been
told that God created her out of his side and called her Eve.

Philo asks: "Do not these seem to you, Sophia, to be very
great discrepancies in the writings of Moses?" Sophia cannot, of
course, but agree with that and considers it inconceivable that
the divine Moses should contradict himself so obviously unless it
was done deliberately. He wished perhaps to imply a mystery
hidden beneath these obvious discrepancies. Philo also thinks
that Moses wished us to realize that he was contradicting himself and to search for his reasons for doing so. Philo explains
that the ordinary commentator wearies himself trying to bring
harmony into the literal text, saying that first it refers in brief
to the creation of both man and woman, then tells in detail how
woman was made from the side of the man. This explanation is
unsatisfactory because of the contradictions in the account.

Leone tries to solve the problem by introducing the idea that
Adam was first male and female. This double-sexed being was
joined at the shoulders and later divided. The philosopher is
here following the rabbinical interpretation, yet with a very remarkable and original variation.

Even within the framework of the concept of Adam containing both sexes, Leone discovers a new meaning in the myth, differing from Plato's speculation. In his view, man sinned only after being divided into two halves not as Plato assumes before. When the two individuals were still linked at the shoulders they could not come together "in the union of the flesh." In this truly admirable and ingenious investigation of the two Genesis narratives Leone is already on the track of an interpretation which he could not complete because he did not have psychoanalytic methods of exploration. Leone penetrated to the core of the problem more than half a millenium before the era of recent scholarly exegesis of the Bible. His inspired survey of Biblical contradictions stands out of the abundance of abstruse and allegorical interpretations and analogies.

It is, in my view, very likely that the myth that primal man contained both sexes is a later development and, as such, a much altered and distorted version of an earlier saga in which a divine couple, god and goddess, are surprised in sexual intercourse and forcefully divided by a son-god. In the late Hebrew legend, Yahweh divides the original human being into two halves by fashioning two faces and two backs. It seems to me that here is the variation of the original situation in which the divine couple have melted into one body by means of sexual intercourse. In it god and goddess created as the French say, "l'animal à deux dos"—the animal with two backs.

The speculations of Leone Ebreo, as well as those of other mystics, convince us that the problem of the double-sexed Adam would not have arisen had the two accounts of man's creation not been compared and contrasted. It was not only the contradictions, so numerous and flagrant, that made those early thinkers search for a solution to the problem, but above and beyond them, the absurd tale of Eve's creation from Adam's rib.

"Each man in his time plays many parts," says Shakespeare. Yet, for Adam simultaneously to play the part of father and mother to a daughter was unacceptable even to the religious Jews and Christians. In this connection the concept of Adam as an androgynous being sounds as if it were an unconscious parody of the Biblical tale. A woman can give birth to a male, but the performance cannot be reversed. There is no two-way street here.

CHAPTER III

ADAM AND THE ANIMALS

IT MIGHT seem that the foregoing chapter oversteps the boundaries of our subject, the interpretation of the Biblical story of the creation of woman from Adam's rib. Yet the discussion was necessary precisely because we would like to draw clear demarcation lines around our problem and to indicate its limits. The shortest distance between two points of relevant material in myth research is rarely a direct line. In cases like this, the straight and narrow path is sometimes not the path of greatest advantage, but that of least intellectual resistance.

The Genesis stories were originally small and independent tales superficially joined and closely knit together only much later. We must separate the account of Eve's creation from the report on the previous part of the Adam story.

The second chapter of Genesis tells us that the Lord said, "It is not good that the man should be alone. I will make him a help-meet for him." There follows the account on the creation of the animals whom the Lord brought unto Adam to see what he would call them. Adam gave names to all the cattle, and to the fowl of the air, and to every beast of the field, but "for Adam there was not found an help-meet for him" (II:20). Only after the failure of that experiment with the animals does God decide to create Eve.

In the Talmudic literature there are, of course, comments about Adam and the beasts too. Rabbi Acha, for instance, says: "When God let the animals pass by Adam, it was in pairs and

Adam cried, "Each forms with its mate a couple, only I not!"[1] The rabbis also raised the question of why the Lord did not create Eve at the same time and together with Adam. The answer to this was: "Because God foresaw that Adam would complain about her. He did not, therefore, create her before Adam asked for her." In this way, the creation of woman was justified. The rabbis decided furthermore that the first man became conscious of sexual desire only after he saw Eve before him.

A different view is expressed only once: in this isolated passage, it is stated that Adam had sexual relations with the animals before Eve was created.[2] There is, it seems no other rabbinical view of a similar kind, and one might conclude that this concept was not widespread among Talmudic commentators.

It was brought to life again, however, as part of Genesis exegesis by modern scholars. Some of them attempted to find a foundation for their view that an old tradition of this kind existed by comparisons with Babylonian and other ancient mythological tales about the beginnings of the world. Almost sixty years ago, Morris Jastrow, professor of Semitic Languages at the University of Pennsylvania, conceived of part of the Babylonian Gilgamesh Epic as a counterpart to that phase of the Biblical story.[3] The epic poem is a composite production in which various tales, originally independent of each other, were joined together. One of the prominent figures in it is Eabani, whom the goddess Aararu created out of earth. If he is not the first man in the world, he is certainly the most primitive one. He is naked, his whole body is covered with hair, and he lives with the beasts.

> . . . eating herbs with gazelles
> Drinking from a trough with cattle
> Sporting with the creatures of the waters.

A sacred prostitute Ukhat ensnares Eabani, who for six days enjoys her love. For six days and seven nights Eabani,

. . . after he had satiated himself with her charms
He returns his countenance to his cattle.
The reposing gazelles saw Eabani
The cattle of the field turned away from him.
Eabani was startled and grew faint
His limbs grew stiff as his cattle ran away.

Jastrow asserts that this part of the epic implies that Eabani had "satisfaction of the sexual passion" through intercourse with the animals before he knew Ukhat. They deserted him only after he had associated with a woman: "They feel that he no longer belongs to them."[4]

Comparing that portion of the Eabani story with the Biblical tale of Adam, who lives first in close communication with the beasts, Jastrow comes to certain conclusions. In his view, the phrase "assigning of names" in Genesis is a veiled expression for sexual intercourse. After Adam assigned names to the animals, he found, says the Biblical narrative, that there was no help meet among them. According to Jastrow, the succession of these statements means that the Biblical writer wants to say in a veiled way that Adam was dissatisfied with the kind of life he led in the company of cattle. In other words, the Yahwist narrative expresses the idea that man felt the unworthiness of his associating with animals.

It was not farfetched to compare Adam's clinging to Eve with Eabani's strong attachment to Ukhat.[5] But Jastrow goes several steps beyond this in interpreting the sentence "Therefore, shall a man leave his father and his mother, and shall cleave unto his wife." The scholar reconstructs an old Hebrew tradition according to which Adam forsakes the animals after encountering Eve. In a later age this tradition had lost its meaning. Time had passed and the stage of belief which had given rise to that legend had also passed. The tradition was thus energetically reshaped. The same tendencies that brought about the veiling of sexual concourse with animals under such a phrase as "assigning names" to them led, in the tradition, to the substitution of father and mother who are deserted for a woman. The original idea is conveyed that man forsook his animal associates upon finding a "mate worthier of him."[6]

In Jastrow's interpretation, the later reader or listener to Adam's story is supposed to feel contempt for Adam and his search for a help meet among the cattle, in the sense of the term: "the company he keeps."

Jastrow considered the lonely situation of the primal man and emphasized his sexual needs. In this version of the Biblical tale Adam's life centers on a perversion. Only after this proves unsatisfactory does Eve, the help meet, appear. The emergency situation in which Adam finds himself reminds the reader of the old story of an isolated farmer in the South who kisses his cow on the forehead saying, "If you could only wash and cook!"

Have we, at last, arrived at a point where we can concentrate our attention on the passages that deal with the myth of woman's creation from Adam's rib? Not yet. To restrict our investigation to these passages—strictly speaking to three verses (Genesis II: 21-23)—would mean to confine our search within too narrow limits since it does not consider post-Biblical sources, which sometimes bring ancient forgotten traditions to the surface, as a river carries surprising objects ashore from its depths.

Even among Jews there is the strange misconception that the post-Biblical literature of Judaism consists mainly of laws, rules and regulations, and of rabbinical commentaries to and explanations of the Torah. Some people go so far as to consider this material unworthy of their attention. In reality the stories, fairy tales and legends of post-Biblical literature are a treasure house of exquisite gems of poetry—often of wit and wisdom. To see in the Bible the end of Jewish literature would be comparable to thinking of Shakespeare's work as the termination of English literature.

Considering the legendary material of the post-Biblical era, especially that which establishes a close connection between the Biblical stories and later creations of Jewish imagination, will serve a twofold purpose. As mentioned before, part of forgotten or disavowed traditions of the people was faithfully preserved in this abundant flow of folklore. Those legends and stories also give us insights into the concept the Jews themselves had of the Biblical narratives and how they explained, enlarged and embroidered them. The peculiar form of the Aggadah was often used by the rabbinic teacher for didactic purposes, particularly to illustrate and illuminate obscure passages and ambiguous meanings of the old legends. It is not astonishing that parts or particles of that rich folklore material are to be found not only in the writings of rabbinical commentators, but also in those of the Gnostics and of the church fathers.

We shall not hesitate to include those later traditions, preserved in the folklore, into the compass of our investigation. What, for instance, do we know about Eve? There is no source about the life of the mother of mankind besides the Holy Scripture. We know nothing about her childhood and early girlhood. We do not even know how old she was when she bore her children, and we do not know at what age she died. We have no information about her married life with Adam except that the favored dessert she served him was fruit. Since there is such scarcity of biographical data, we shall also welcome rumors, legends and other unauthenticated material.

In addition to other characteristic features, that old folklore material shows a very great tenacity and longevity. Freud found the explanation of some strange elements of one of his dreams in a memory reaching back into his sixth year.[7] The little boy was then told by his mother that all men are made of dust and must therefore return to dust. This did not please the child, and he doubted that it was correct. Then his mother rubbed the palms of her hands together—just as in making dumplings, except that there was no dough between them—and showed him the blackish scales of epidermis formed thereby. This was meant to be a proof that we are made of dust. The astonishment of little Sigmund at this "demonstration ad oculos" was enormous, and he accepted the idea which I was later to hear expressed in the words "Thou owest nature a death."

It was very likely that Freud's mother—I still knew the old lady—had heard of that proof demonstrating the story of Adam's creation in the Hassidic circles in which she grew up in Brody, Galicia. Comparisons and allusions of this kind, as well as tales and legends referring to Biblical persons and events, are continuations of the rich heritage of Jewish folklore of the Middle Ages. It is appropriate to add a few features to the picture of Adam as it is painted by later commentators.

The rabbis asserted that Adam was born circumcised since he was created in God's own image.[8] Rabbi Judah B. R. Simon declared that Adam and Eve were created at the age of twenty years.[9] The wisdom and the enormous stature of our remotest kinsman plays an important part in the view of some Talmudists, as well as in the opinion of many Gnostic sects. Rabbi Akiba asserts that the angels, noticing Adam's resemblance to God, asked: "Are there two powers in the world?" God then reduced Adam's size, which had formerly filled the entire universe, to one cubit.[10] A psychoanalytically-trained Biblical scholar will easily recognize a displaced symbol of castration in the reduction of Adam's size. The same purpose of denial is served by the saga that the first man was a gigantic monster without life or intelligence before the Lord animated him.

According to some passages of rabbinic literature, God created man without a soul and then created the animals. If he had received his soul before all other creatures were formed, man could have been considered God's assistant in creation. As can easily be seen, here all possibility of another God-like creature is thus carefully ruled out. More than one feature of Jewish folklore points to a disavowed original tradition that Adam was conceived as a divine or superhuman being—quite in accord with the cosmologies of the Babylonians, Egyptians and other people of the ancient Orient. Under the pressure of monotheistic Yahwism, this original character of the primal being had to be radically changed. It was necessary to reduce not only his stature, but also his status.

CHAPTER IV

THE RABBIS

LEGENDS say that creation itself was preceded by the profound reflections of the Maker about the material to be used in his production. The Lord considered, for instance,[1] the possible consequences of his choice for the nature of woman and said: "I will not make her from the head of man, lest she carry her head high in arrogant pride; not from the eye, lest she be wanton-eyed; not from the ear, lest she will be an eavesdropper; not from the neck, lest she will be insolent; not from the mouth, lest she will be a tattler; not from the heart, lest she be inclined to envy; not from the hand, lest she be a meddler; not from the foot, lest she be a gadabout. I will form her from a chaste part of the body." As He then formed every limb and organ, God said: "Be chaste! Be chaste!"

The French have a proverb proclaiming that what woman wants is the Will of God (*Ce que veut la femme, Dieu le veut*). It is obvious that the sentence cannot always be reversed. At least in the case of Eve's creation, God's wish remained a pious one. As the rabbis assure us, in spite of the caution used by the Creator, she had all the faults which God tried to avoid. The daughters of Eve were haughty and insolent and wanton-eyed. Sarah was an eavesdropper when the angel spoke with Abraham; Miriam was a talebearer when she accused Moses; and Rachel was envious of her sister, Leah. And did not Eve take the forbidden fruit?

The differences of the sexes were sometimes explained by the divergence of their origin. Why, it is asked, is it that man walks facing the earth while woman looks upwards? Man glances at the place of his creation and so does woman.[2] The Levite Rabbi Joshua ben Hananiah, who was born at the time of Pontius Pilot, taught that woman's defects were an inheritance from Eve. He was asked why it is harder to pacify a woman than a man, and he answered: "Men were created from dust and it softens at once. But Eve was created from bone; though you pour on bone any amount of water, it will not soften it."

Biblical exegesis was used to explain other differences of the sexes. Why does woman perfume herself? Man was created from dust which does not putrefy. But woman, born from bone, would lose her savor if she did not perfume herself, just as meat putrefies without spices. Why is a woman's voice shrill compared with that of a man? When soft viands are cooked, no sound is heard, but a bone, put in a pot, begins to crackle. Why is it the man who does the wooing and not the woman? Because the man seeks what he has lost, but woman does not seek him since she is taken from him.

When Adam first saw Eve, he was full of enthusiasm for her. It was both the first love in the world and also love at first sight. The rabbis tell us that Eve was full of beauty and grace. God had, in the eighth hour of the sixth day of creation, adorned her with the splendor of the bride. He led Adam under a series of canopies studded with gems and pearls and ornamented with gold. The archangels Michael and Gabriel acted as groomsmen. After the ceremony at which God pronounced the blessings, the angels danced in the Garden beating their timbrels and singing songs.[3]

The rabbis report that God, who gave Eve away, adorned her with wimples and bracelets and earrings and rings on her hands, as well as with tinkling ornaments on her feet. The Bible says of the couple that "they were both naked, the man and the wife, and were not ashamed" (Gen. II:25). Logically, no trousseau is mentioned.

All was wonderful at first, and the couple felt as if they were in Paradise. Only later did Adam become aware that there was a worm in the apple—or whatever the forbidden fruit was. Only later, and too late, did Adam recognize that he was led up the garden path, if there was one in the Garden of Eden. This is, at least, the tenor of many of the post-Biblical writers' comments.

Did this misogynous tendency really emerge so late? Was not an attitude of hostility or hatred already palpable in the original tale? It is difficult to deny that the great writer who reported the creation of Eve was not an admirer of women. Frazer, who praises his artistic qualities, says of him[4] that he "hardly attempted to hide his deep contempt of women. The lateness of her creation and the irregular and undignified manner of it—made out of a piece of her lord and master after all the lower animals had been created in a regular and decent manner—sufficiently mark the low opinion he held of her nature. . . ."

It is remarkable how few writers commenting on the Genesis myth of Eve's creation have felt its scarcely concealed hostility to woman although, as Frazer remarks, the misogyny of the Yahwist "takes a still darker tinge when he ascribes all the misfortunes and sorrows of the human race to the credulous folly and unbridled appetite of its first mother."

There are, however, some stories in the Jewish tradition which show that women could promptly reply to open and concealed attacks upon them. Among the many charming little gems of the Talmud, which if collected would be a glittering bracelet, is the story of a conversation between the Emperor and the daughter of Rabbi Gamaliel. The Emperor remarked to the Rabbi:[5] "Your God is a thief, for it is written 'And the Lord God caused a deep sleep to fall upon Adam and he slept and He took one of his ribs. . .' " Thereupon his daughter said to him: "Let me answer him." Turning to the Emperor, she requested: "Give me an officer!" (meaning a police inspector). "What for?" he asked.

She said: "Thieves visited us last night and robbed us of a silver pitcher, leaving a golden one in its place!" "I wish," he exclaimed, "such thieves would visit us every day." "Ah!" she retorted, "was it not Adam's gain that he was deprived of a rib and given a wife instead to serve him?"

The discussion does not end with this poignant comparison, because the Emperor went on to say: "That is what I mean. He should have taken the rib from him openly when Adam was awake." And she answered: "Let me have a piece of raw meat!" When it was brought, she placed it under her armpit, then took it out and offered it to him. "It makes my stomach turn," he objected. "Even so would Eve have been repulsive to Adam, had she been taken from him openly." In another version of the same theme, a matron asks Rabbi Jose[6] why God created woman while Adam slept. Rabbi Jose replied: "He first created her before his eyes, but since he saw her full of slime and blood, God separated her from Adam and created her again."

It is interesting that Adam's sleep is in some sources considered proof that the first man was only human. The angels first thought that Adam was the Lord of all and were ready to salute him with "Holy, holy, holy is the Lord of hosts!" when God caused sleep to fall upon him and then all creatures recognized the difference between God and men.[7] With reference to a possible creation of Eve in Adam's presence, the sages explain that had Adam watched Eve's creation, she would not have awakened love in him and would even have repelled him: "To this day it is true that men do not appreciate the charms of women whom they have known and observed from childhood on."[8]

When Adam roused himself from his profound sleep and saw Eve in all her beauty before him, he exclaimed: "This is she who caused my heart to throb many a night." Rabbi Simon ben Lakisch declared that this anticipation of Eve makes dreams so fatiguing for men because Adam enjoyed intimacy with Eve in his dreams.[9]

The misogynous tendency in most rabbinical comments on the creation story is so pervasive that it can already be felt in the discussion about the preparatory steps leading to Eve's emergence. The enthusiasm with which Adam greeted her when he awakened did not prevent him from quickly discerning what her real nature was. He foresaw that she would carry her point with man by entreaties and tears, or flattery and caresses. He said, therefore, "This is my never-silent bell."[10]

It is as if the rabbis had anticipated the malicious lines an unknown author wrote many centuries later:

> Whilst Adam slept,
> Eve from his side arose.
> Strange! His first sleep
> Should be his last repose!

CHAPTER V

BONE OF CONTENTION

IT WOULD be a mistake to assume that the hairsplitting discussions about Eve's creation can be found only in late Jewish literature and are a manifestation of a genuine Talmudic way of thinking. You will find quite similar discussions in the works of the great scholastic Peter Lombard who was Bishop of Paris and taught there at the Dominican school. In his main work, *Libri quatuor Sententiarum* (1150-1152), for instance, he explored the question of why Adam slept during the creation of Eve, since the importance of the event would have well justified his being awake. Besides other ensnaring questions, such as where God was before the creation of the world, the famous theologian asked why the rib and no other part of the body was chosen by the Lord when He created Eve. Yes, Lombard even dares to reflect upon the problem of why the first pair was not produced in the usual manner, doubtless as popular then as now.

The misogynous tendency in the rabbis can be found again in the Christian literature of the scholastics. A scholarly treatise entitled *Disputatio Nova,* published in 1595, tries to prove that women are not human beings. Since God is omniscient, He must have known that He would create Eve. If He wanted her to be human like Adam, He would not have used the singular saying, "I want to make man."[1]

Samuel Butler wrote in *Hudibras* (Pt. I, canto 173), published in 1663:

He knew the seat of Paradise. . . .
What Adam dreamt of when his bride
Came from the closet of his side . . .
If either of them had a navel

The German physician, Christian Tobias Ephraim, in Camenz in 1752 was still exploring the question of whether our primal ancestors, Adam and Eve, had a navel and came to the conclusion that they didn't because they were not born but created. In his book, published in Hamburg, he wrote, "Whoever doubts this is no worthy member of the church and should be delivered to the Devil."

It was fortunate that the founder of modern anatomy, Andreas Vesalius (1514-1564), escaped this terrible fate. This famous man was professor of surgery at Padua and later at Bologna and Basel. In his time the doctrine was accepted that every man had one rib less on one side than on the other since Eve had been taken from man's rib. But Vesalius and his students asserted that man had the same number of ribs as woman. Vesalius was charged with dissecting a living human being. On a pilgrimage to the Holy Land he was shipwrecked and lost to the world in the prime of his life.[2]

The rib in the Genesis narrative was thus in the center of the lore about Eve and in more than one sense became a bone of contention. Bossuet (1627-1704) still depicted Eve as made from a "supernumerary" bone of Adam.

The Hebrew word for rib (tsela) remained the object of various exegeses. It was often translated as side. It is still uncertain when and where the interpretation first cropped up that the word which usually meant rib sometimes meant a tail. Some rabbi explained the Genesis story according to the Psalm's verse "Behind and before hast thou formed me" and came to the conclusion that Adam had a tail. The rabbis brought this view into harmony with the sentence that God made the rib into a woman and closed up the flesh where the bone had been removed.[3] It seems that in only one passage of the Talmud is the word used in Genesis for rib interpreted as tail.[4] Yet the interpretation became popular in the Middle Ages.

There are, they say, distinctions without differences. The transformation of the rib into a tail in folklore does not belong to that category since the change implied a degradation of the woman, as can clearly be shown in the later development of the lore about Eve. From many stories preserved in Germany, Bulgaria, Russia and other countries, we can recognize how, in the popular imagination, the creation of the first woman from a tail came about.[5] In some of those fables Satan plays a sinister part, but in most cases the dog is the villain. In a story in Styria, the dog stole the rib and ran away with it. God chased him and could only catch his tail, from which he later fashioned woman. In Russia people felt that Adam had a tail like an ape which God cut off to create woman.

Hans Sachs, the most prominent German poet of the sixteenth century, in 1557 wrote a long narrative poem in which he described how God put aside the rib of dormant Adam and pasted the wound over with earth. While He washed the blood from His hands, the dog stole the rib. God then cut off the dog's tail from which he formed Eve. In the poet's ungallant view, three things remind us of that ignoble origin of woman: as a dog flatters us with wagging his tail when he wants something, so woman caresses us when she desires a thing; when she cannot get it, she begins to bark; and finally, she has inherited fleas from the dog's tail.

With the mention of Hans Sachs' versified account of Eve, we have already entered the realm of poetry dedicated to the creation of woman and its consequences. The subject is deserving of special treatment.

CHAPTER VI

THE POETS

IT IS no wonder that the imagination of writers and poets has always been fired by the biblical story of Eve's creation as well as by the whimsical traditions of it in later times. The New York Public Library possesses a rare booklet intitled *Adam's Tail or The First Metamorphosis*, dated 1774,[1] which describes the strange happenings of woman's first emergence. It begins thus:

> When Jove, as learned Rabbins say,
> Had form'd our common Sir of Clay,
> Had spun the Nerves, sublim'd the Juices,
> And giv'n each Part its various Uses,
> To grace the Monarch's princely Thighs,
> And guard his royal Side from Flies
> That might his tender Flesh assail,
> He furnished Adam with a Tail.

In the following lines, the anonymous poet turns directly to women:

> For trust me, Ladies, if you think,
> That tails were only made to stink,
> If your ideas of them be
> Not full of Grace and Dignity,
> Attend and it shall soon be shown
> The Fault's not Nature's, but your own.

The ladies are then reminded of peacocks, proud of their tails, of squirrels in their cages and other animals with tails. God,

who saw Adam's lifeless tail, decided to transform it into a
woman. Thus, woman is a tail in masquerade:

> In this new Form may still depend
> On Adam as an humble Friend,
> Still serve his Pleasure, mark his Will
> And solace his Posteriors still.

To vouch for the veracity of woman's creation, the author
refers to authorities witnessing the old tradition:

> Thus say the Rabbins, Men who knew
> Scripture as well as we can do
> They say not Moses told a Fib
> In drawing Eve from Adam's rib,
> But, that through Ignorance of their Tongue
> Divines translate the Passage wrong
> And that the Septuagint imposes
> A tale on us, not told by Moses.

He refers to many proofs from history and various contemporary sources. They all allude

> . . . to that Part allied
> Which Mankind always strive to Hide
> Full many a Sage of rev'rend Beard
> Has said; Maid, never should be heard,
> Which proves they drew their Birth from thence
> Where every Whisper gives offence.

After this and other vulgar allusions, the writer continues to
contribute "proofs" for his theory of woman's origin:

> When Men are marry'd, Fate adorns
> Their lordly Forehead oft with Thorns
> And where's the Beast o'er Hill or Dale
> That carries Thorns without a Tail?
> The Truth is this, to end all strife
> The Tail we look for—is the Wife

Plato's famous fable of the androgynous primal being is wrong,
thus:

> May we not fairly end our Pages
> With this great Truth, for future Ages
> And future Nations to believe?
> 'T was Adams Tail that now is Eve.
> Thus, Ladies, I have told my Story
> And laid some modest Proofs before you—
> A slave to Beauty's mild Dominion.
> And old Tradition I've related
> A few Conjectures simply stated
> Can shew my Author's Page and Place
> And leave yourselves to judge the Case
> Well knowing, if we disagree
> You'll blame the Rabbins and not me.

It is unlikely that the Irish poet Thomas Moore knew this versified attack on women when about fifty years later he wrote a little piece on the same subject. He must, however, have known the same unsavory source of the saga since he refers to it.[2]

> They tell us that woman was made of a rib
> Just picked from a corner so smug in the side;
> But the Rabbins swear to you that this is a fib
> And 'twas not so at all that the sex was supplied.
> The Old Adam was fashioned, the first of his kind,
> With a tail like a monkey, full yard and a span
> And then nature cut off his appendage behind,
> Why, then woman was made of the tail of the man.
> If such is the tie between woman and man,
> The ninny who weds is a pitiful elf.
> For he takes to his tail, like an idiot again,
> And makes a most damnable ape of himself.
> Yet if we may judge as the fashion prevails
> Every husband remembers the original plan
> And knowing his wife is no more than his tail
> Why, he leaves her behind him as much as he can.

There are many other pieces of coarse and doubtful humor alluding to the tradition of Adam's tail, but the samples quoted here will suffice to prove the tenacity of folklore of this kind.

Poets were also more or less seriously dealing with the other tradition relating to Eve as fashioned from Adam's rib: In Milton's *Paradise Lost*, Adam speaks:

> To give thee being, I lent
> Out of my side life to thee, nearest my heart. . . .

The lines in which Adam declares his love for his mate are devastatingly funny:

> How can I live without thee,
>   how forego
> Thy sweet converse and Love, . . .
>   so dearly joined
> To live again in those wild
>   Woods forlorn?
> Should God create another Eve
>   and I
> Another Rib afford, yet Loss of thee
> Would never from my Heart . . .

(*Paradise Lost,* 6. K, IX, 906)

Such expressions of passionate emotion, to be found in the works of the great poets of the seventeenth century, are utterly incompatible with the taste and tact of our time. Compare for instance Laertes' lament over the body of his drowned sister,

> Too much of water hast thou, poor Ophelia,
> And therefore I forbid my tears.
>   (HAMLET, Act IV, 7)

Goethe let his Oriental mouthpiece, the Persian poet Hafiz, speak:

> For woman due allowance make
> Formed of a crooked rib was she—
> For Heaven could not straightened be.
> Attempt to bend her, and she'll break.
> If let alone, more crooked grows.
> What well could be Madame worse,
> My good friend Adam?—
> For woman due allowance make
> 'Twere grievous, if the rib would break.

In Samuel Taylor Coleridge's *Epigrams* there are a few lines in which woman is identified with the rib:

> "What? Rise again with all one's bones?"
> Quoth Gilles: "I hope you fib
> I trusted when I went to Heaven
> To go without my rib."

As recently as our own time, the rib as the birthplace of Eve is mentioned. One of Barrie's characters in *What Every Woman Knows* remarks: "You see, dear, it is not true that woman was made from man's rib; she was really made from his funny bone."

And Alexander Pope calls up the vision of Adam's loneliness:

> Our grandsire, ere of Eve possess'd
> With mournful looks the blissful scene surveyed,
> And wander'd in the solitary shade,
> The Maker saw, took pity and bestow'd
> Woman, the last, the best reserv'd by God

A contemporary American poet, Karl Shapiro[3] presents Adam as feeling labor in his bone. God explains to him: "This sickness in your skeleton is longing. I will remove it from your clay." It begins to rain; God sits down beside sick Adam:

> ... When he was fast asleep
>   He wet his right hand deep in Adam's side
>   And drew the graceful rib out of his breast ...

Voices in defense of woman as made from man's rib are few and far between. The scornful Lady in Beaumont and Fletcher's comedy speaks:

> Woman they say, was made of man.
> Me thinks 'tis strange; they should be so unlike;
> It may be all the best was cut away
> To make the woman, and then naught was left
> Behind with him.

The same view emerges in the prologue to John Dryden's *Amphytrion*:

Our sex, you know, was after your's designed
The last Perfection of the Maker's Mind.
Heaven drew out all the Gold for us
And left our Dross behind.

One has to skip almost two hundred years to find lines in poetry
favorably mentioning Eve's mysterious creation from a rib. In
a letter by Elizabeth Crawford, part of a song is quoted which
Abraham Lincoln used to sing. It was written to Sarah Haggard
on her marriage to Grisby,[4] and is entitled "Adam and Eve's
Wedding Song." It contains the stanzas:

This woman was not taken
From Adam's feet, we see,
So he must not abuse her,
The meaning seems to be.
This woman was not taken
From Adam's head, we know
To show, she must not rule him
'Tis evidently so.
This woman, she was taken
From under Adam's arm.
So she must be protected
From injury and harm.

I do not remember any longer which modern writer arrived
at the original explanation of Eve's creation which maintained
that God, in His wisdom, foresaw that Adam would be unable
to take care of himself.

The lore around Yahweh, Adam and Eve, as it appears in
the rabbinical literature and in poetry is, so to speak, the statue
crowned portal through which we enter the house of modern
Biblical interpretation.

CHAPTER VII

TOO-SMOOTH SAILING

BACK IN 1891 and in the years following, the eminent German critic, Alfred Kerr often discussed the realistic plays of that time[1] and once pointed out that an everyday event in life and the same everyday event on the stage often have very different effects on those present. It happens hundreds of times in life that someone speaks of a person, characterizing him as "funny," and at the very same moment that person opens the door saying exactly the funny thing just quoted. This is a quite frequent occurrence; yet when it occurs on the stage, every listener considers it contrived. Another example: it often happens in actual life that a middle-aged man at the dinner table with his family suddenly has a stroke and drops dead. The same event has no dramatic effect in a play, unless it has been carefully prepared for in the minds of the audience. In other words, if that event comes as a pure accident and surprise and is not at least unconsciously expected, it will affect us only as a shock. It works quite differently upon us if, for instance, a friend of the family casually remarks in the first act that the man has a weak heart and has to be careful, or a physician warns his wife that he has to avoid great excitement because of his heart condition. Yes, the effect will be even stronger if a reminder of such a kind is repeated and then, after a longer time (let us say, in a scene of conflict in the third act), he suddenly feels ill and dies. The strong effect is prepared for, though the event came by surprise. It was unconsciously expected. If we are not fore-

warned, the shock will be there, but not the effect desired by
the playwright. The surprise will be as dull as that experienced
when a chest of drawers suddenly collapses. An audience which
is fully unprepared and sees on the stage the head of the house
suddenly sink down dead, will not feel the fear and pity Aristotle
would demand from the tragedy.

I have often wondered how an audience would react if Hamlet,
taking his constitutional after dinner on the battlements of
Elsinore with his friend Horatio, suddenly ran into his father's
ghost. It is unlikely that the dramatic effect of such an encounter
could be nearly as profound as it is after we are prepared by
Horatio's tale. When you follow the first scenes of the tragedy,
you recognize that the suspense is artificially increased and pro-
longed. Even when the ghost appears, he does not immediately
begin to talk.

We cannot believe in a miracle, if we are not prepared for it.
Only that which tantalizes us, or gives us time to wonder, can
become a mystery for us. All other things might have the effect
of shock, might take us and shake us by surprise, and leave us
bewildered, stupid or confused, but they are not felt as mysterious. Where nothing is concealed, no revelation is expected.

Once we are psychologically prepared and have accepted the
mysterious or even the miraculous, we no longer doubt that new
miracles can occur. After we have, tentatively, acknowledged
that the old King's ghost appeared to his son, we take his re-
appearance in the Queen's chamber for granted. When you have
accepted one miracle, the second does not present so great a
problem. A visitor at Lourdes who accepts as true that the Holy
Virgin, to whom a patient had dedicated a heart made of gold,
cured his cardiac illness will not doubt that the Mother of God
can make a helpless paralytic walk again. Only an embittered
unbeliever like Anatole France, looking at the votive offerings
in the chapel, will wonder why there are no crutches there. The
Bible reader who believes that the Lord said, "Let there be

light," and there was light, will not refuse to believe that the Lord made the firmament and divided the waters.

We read the Genesis chapters as the story of the beginning of the creation and are not astonished to learn that Adam begat a son when he was a hundred and thirty years old and that he lived afterwards for eight hundred years. Nor are we shocked when we read of the days of Enoch, Cain and Methuselah, who all lived hundreds of years. By no means the smallest share of this willing gullibility from readers is due to the power of Biblical diction. Accustomed to its suggestive sweep, we read, "And it came to pass . . ." and we are ready to believe an utterly incredible tale, as though we were children listening to a father's voice.

In a posthumously published letter, Arthur Schnitzler speaks of the average reader, whom he calls a "curious creature."[2] Let us imagine, he says, that a famous historian writes, "Methuselah became *only* nine hundred and sixty-nine years old," and the average reader will say, "Gosh, how young that fellow was when he died!" The awe in which we hold the author of the Scripture who, if he is not God, wrote divine prose, makes us as ready to believe the account of Eve's birth from Adam's side as we are to accept the appearance of Hamlet's father. We are not blocked because we do no longer wonder.

There are two kinds of acceptance of the mysterious: that of the naive believer and that of the naive disbeliever. The figure of the sphinx at Thebes was no object of wonder for the Egyptian of the time of the XX Dynasty. He was not astonished when he saw that there was a creature half-man, half-lion. But also the average American tourist is not intrigued by the sphinx; he or she considers it "cute" or "funny," and that's that.

The Genesis story contains nothing astonishing for the fundamentalist. It is as readily accepted as any other Biblical account —for instance, the story of the Egyptian army drowning in the Red Sea through which the Israelites passed safely. But the modern Biblical commentator also sees nothing baffling in the tale of Eve's creation from Adam's side. Here is a piece of old folklore, no different from any other to be found in the Old Testament; a just-so story.

To the modern Biblical commentator that account appears simply as a fairly tale without any deeper significance. He is as little inclined to muse over it as over the witch who wants to eat Hansel and Gretel. The Genesis story of Eve's birth is as primitive a myth as Snow White is a primitive fairy tale, and a mythologist knows what a myth is like.

"Is there no meaning in myths at all?" someone may ask. Of course there is significance in them and a very different kind from that found in fairy tales. Children believe in fairy tales; the members of primitive tribes believe in myths which are supposed to describe the vicissitudes of their tribal ancestors. In the case of the creation myth the earliest history of primeval mankind is presented. The ancient peoples believed in the truth of the myths the way pious Jews of our own day are convinced that the Torah was given to Moses on Mount Sinai, or a faithful Christian believes that Christ is the Son of God crucified and resurrected on the third day.

There are, of course, other differences between myths and fairy tales. Fairy tales are amusing or entertaining pieces of fiction, but myths have a definite meaning. What meaning? They assign a cause or various causes to a given phenomenon. They explain how it came about. They are aetiological. A little boy examining Swiss cheese asks, "What are the holes for?" or wonders, "Where does the light go when it is turned off?" The answer to the second question should explain to him the nature of electricity and the devices charged with electricity. In the same sense, we are told, myths explain the origin and essence of natural phenomena and social institutions.

We have already had some examples of such aetiological explanations: God put Adam into a deep sleep before that operation because the Lord's work does not tolerate an observer. But are such explanations produced only by medieval theologians? Not at all. Many modern scholars find solutions here for quite a few obscure passages of the Holy Scripture. An instance is S. R. Driver who has no doubt that there is profound significance in the report of Eve's being taken from Adam's body: "The moral and social relations of the sexes to each other, the dependence of woman upon man, her close relationship to him and the foundation existing in nature for the attachment springing up between them. . . . the feeling with which each should naturally regard the other."[3] In explanation of that enigmatic tale, we are told that "It is the wife's natural duty to be at hand, ready at all times to be a 'help' to her husband, as it is the husband's natural duty . . . to cherish and defend his wife as part of his own self."[4] That is, in this commentator's view, the explanation or, if you like, the meaning of the myth of Eve being taken from Adam's side. Thus, the verse, "Therefore shall a man leave his father and mother and shall cleave unto his wife"—clearly the gloss of a very late editor or scribe of the text—is explained as the foundation of marriage and, moreover, of monogamous marriage "as the direct consequence of a relation established by the Creator."

A whole school of Biblical commentators has taken over such aetiological explanations of the Eve saga. Only recently Gerhard von Rade characterized that last sentence as "a short epilogue after the curtain fell."[5] Von Rade, who at least admits that this was the narrator's purpose, states that the whole story reached the essential target toward which it was aimed right from the beginning of the sentence. Here it shows "what it really wants; its aetiological character." To von Rade, then, the story indicates that it departed in search of an answer to the question of where the powerful drive of the sexes toward each other comes from and concludes that it exists because woman is taken from man, that once they were originally one flesh.

The idea that the Eve story seeks to explain the institution of monogamous marriage is exceedingly funny even when one

does not consider that the patriarchs had several wives. Even the
Interpreters' Bible admits that the verse which speaks of man's
cleaving unto his wife was the addition of a later writer and did
not originally present an affirmation that marriage was from the
beginning monogamous by divine intention. Such an affirmation
would indeed "have been impossible at this time," the commentator concludes with praiseworthy restraint.[6]

Studying the comments of Biblical scholars who explain the
myth of Eve's creation in such an aetiological way leads to the
impression that half-nomadic desert tribes were concerned with
the problem of the origin of monogamous marriage. A saga of
primitive character is presented from the viewpoint of a sermon
delivered from the pulpit of a church or synagogue. An aetiological interpretation of this kind is a pandemonium of rationalism
where common sense runs amuck.

Modern criticism sees no secret, no mystery in the Biblical
story of Eve's birth—only a myth. A glance at some medieval
paintings—even at Michelangelo's fresco in the Sistine Chapel
—communicates a different impression. If there is no enigma
there, there is at least a rebus, the representation of a meaning
by way of a picture.

The progress made in understanding the sacred text branched
off at the point of the aetiological concept of myths and bravely
marched along a misleading path. One begins to wonder why
the saga following the report of Eve's creation could not be interpreted in an aetiological manner. It could, for instance, explain certain phases of the married life of Adam and Eve. As
far as I know, no serious Biblical scholar has yet interpreted the
paradise as a honeymoon or the expulsion from Eden as the
end of the sweet illusion of love.

CHAPTER VIII

THE COMMENTATORS

BIBLICAL SCHOLARS again and again explore the text of the Holy Scripture and show us the many alterations to which it was subjected. These changes, made by editors and scribes, were often omissions and distortions of words and sentences, but sometimes also additions and accretions to the text. The scholars make it appear very likely that most of those alterations of the oral tradition, which was transmitted from the early phases, were determined by the progress in religious and social evolution. The influence of Yahwism and the exclusion of all paganism and pagan mythology is, of course, the most important factor in the reshaping of traditions. One must not forget that the Yahwistic religion introduced to and imposed on the Hebrew tribes was a revolution and was victorious only after long conflict. Orthodoxy is, as a Huguenot pastor once remarked, a heresy that has become successful.

It seems to me that remnants of original Hebrew beliefs, misunderstood or not understood at all, continued to lead a subterranean existence within the Yahwistic world. Disguised as genuine and legitimate parts of the new religion that Moses imposed upon his people in the desert, older Hebrew sagas and customs were preserved in a monotheistic masquerade, so to speak. A tale such as the Biblical saga of Eve's creation from Adam's rib is in its whimsicality a piece of grotesque mythological fantasy which hardly suits its cosmological surrounding. Here is an isolated rock from another geological era in the midst of the Yahwistic stratum, certainly more primitive than the stories of creation from Egyptian, Babylonian and Greek mythology with which it has so often been compared.

Those comparisons, however informative they are, only show that similar features can be traced back to common inheritance. They cannot explain the special form and content of the Biblical saga. Some of the common characteristics demonstrated by the commentators are so obvious and crude that an honest investigator is almost ashamed to call them "similarities."

It is a long way from the primal traditions of the Hebrew tribes to the narratives which the Yahwistic writers collected and arranged—a way longer than that from the tongue to the parchment.[1] My aim is to reconstruct that primal tradition or, more modestly, to define the soil from which the Eve saga grew and then to show which tendencies molded its shape. The marauding tribes that swarmed out of the Arabian deserts into the Fertile Crescent certainly had a body of traditions which they brought with them when they broke into the highly-developed civilizations between the Tigris and the Euphrates. Biblical scholars have not given enough consideration to the fact that the tribes themselves had crude conceptions of the origin of mankind, stories resembling those of Australian aborigines before Christian missionaries taught them the Biblical narratives. The myth of Eve's creation from Adam's body is a late and secondary result of the development of older traditions which belonged to those nomadic tribes who many centuries later were welded into Israel. In other words, the core of the Eve saga originates in the Stone Age and has its roots in a historical phase antedating the incursion of Hebrew tribes into Palestine.

The alterations and modifications of the text which Biblical criticism investigates belong, compared to the early phase which interests us here, to a very recent stage. In opposition to other explorers, we conceive of the transformations of the original myth under the influence of Yahwism as an end result. The Genesis story is for us—whatever its original form was—already as remote from the primal tradition as a Chippendale chair is from the stump of a tree.

How have earlier and modern scholarship interpreted the creation story? A rapid and condensed survey of the explanations of the Eve myth must, of course, depart from the post-Biblical Jewish interpretation of the Genesis narrative. Judaism had soon become a literary religion and all study was at first concentrated on interpretation of the Book of Books. We have already noted the comments and commentaries in which the rabbis of the Talmudic age tried to formulate what was in their view the significance of the story of Eve's creation. Even in our telescopic presentation it was obvious that in the beginning their interpretation of the Genesis saga amounted to reshaping and refashioning it. The literal view was soon replaced by an allegorical concept of the saga. Yet the Pharisaic school declared that the story of the Garden of Paradise was true to fact, exact and historical. The fundamentalist concept of the Eve story remained, of course, unchanged from the early times of Jewish theologians to the present.

The Jewish-Greek philosopher Philo of Alexandria (50 B.C. to 50 A.D.), while not the originator, was the most prominent representative of allegorical exegesis of the Bible which he interpreted in the sense of a mystery religion. In his view Adam and Eve mean reason and sensuality. Many church fathers, for example Origen, and in part also Augustine, followed the path of the allegorical interpretations. Athanasius, Crysostom, Tertullian and others tried to build a bridge from the historical to the allegorical concept.

The Syrian-Hebrew encyclopedist Bar-Hebraeus (c. 1286) declared that the Lord put Adam to sleep so he would not feel pain when the rib was taken from him "because pain is the cause of hatred."[2] Similar views about this particular feature of the creation story are already found in early Talmudic comments[3] and emerge much later as well.

We find the same interpretation almost six hundred years

later in James Y. Simpson's "Answer to the Religious Objections Advanced against the Employment of Anaesthetic in Midwifery and Surgery," published in Edinburgh in 1847. The excellent physician writes with irrefutable logic:[4] "Beside those who urge, on a kind of religious ground, that an artificial or anaesthetic state of unconsciousness should not be induced . . . forget that we have the greatest of all examples set before us for following out this very principle of practice. I allude to that most singular prescription of the preliminaries and details of the first surgical operation ever performed. . . ."

In the verses of the second chapter of Genesis, the author finds the whole process of surgical operation described, but especially striking is that passage dealing with the removal of Adam's rib because it affords "evidence of our Creator Himself using means to save poor human nature from unnecessary enduring of physical pain." We now know what this first performance of an operation under anesthesia was. The context leaves no doubt about the fact that the anesthesia saved Adam from labor pain. The anesthesia that the Lord applied was thus a kind of twilight sleep.

The James Y. Simpson who presented that original argument in defense of anesthesia was almost a contemporary of Johann Gottfried Eichhorn, a professor at Jena (1752-1852). He treated the Biblical story of Eve in a historical and critical sense. He called the Adam-Eve saga a colorful picture of the first emergence of man on earth. The first human beings wandered about, each alone, in the wonderful garden which God had planted for them. Adam, who had been filled with longing for a companion, fell into a deep sleep in which he dreamed that a rib was taken from his side and he was divided into two parts. When he awoke, he saw a woman standing beside him and joyfully took her as his companion.

Eichhorn's *Historisch-Kritische Einleitung in das Alte Testament*[5] was soon followed by books by von Hummelauer,[6] Gottfried Hoberg,[7] O. P. Lagrange[8] and others who presented similar

views of the Eve myth. Hoberg, for instance,[9] states, that Adam
had a vision of Eve after he had recognized that there was no
help meet for him among the animals. The excision of a rib and
the creation from it is, for this commentator, "a visionary process
of a symbolic kind." Its symbolism is similar to that of the
presentations of the church fathers who say that the church was
created from the side of Christ. In this way Chrysostom explained that as Christ built the church from his side, so Eve
emerged from Adam.

It is worth noting the strange conceptions of the Adam-Eve
saga as the mythologists at the beginning of this century saw it.
To explain the Genesis narratives, a certain school of mythologists—under the influence of Babylonian discoveries—reached
for the moon in their interpretations of the Bible. I mean the
kind of interpretation that sees in mythological elements phe-
nomenal processes of nature such as changes in the orbits of the
sun, the moon and the stars, eclipses and so on. This pan-Baby-
lonian school will, for instance, cite the possibility that the name
of Samson can be associated with the sun in Hebrew and conceives of the Biblical Samson story as a decayed solar myth.
It is then not farfetched to say that it follows that the hair in
which the hero's strength lay represented sun-rays. Instead of
discussing the interpretations of Eduard Stucken, Hugo Winkler,
Alfred Jeremias and others, I will quote only a sample of such
moonstruck explanations. For Ernst Böklin there can be no
doubt that the Biblical Adam is a moon-being and that Adamah
(the Hebrew for *earth*) from which he is taken is the female
moon.[10] The creation of woman from man is a "fantastic and
absurd tale" which can only be understood in the sense that the
best completion of one part of the moon is the other half. Woman
was created from a rib, which means, of course, the crescent-
moon, while the creation of animals delineates the emergence of
the stars.

Setting aside the astral-mythological interpretations, we approach the modern concepts, founded on historical comparative and anthropological considerations. We expect information and insight from the experts in Biblical archeology and Semitic folk- lore which only scientific exploration and cool, objective investi- gation can provide. We hope that these scholars will dissect and resolve the mystery of Eve's creation. Not baffled and bewildered by the labyrinthine tale, and understanding ancient oriental thought, the Biblical scholars will, we hope, solve the puzzle.

Of course it is impossible to present here even a condensed report of the numerous interpretations contained in many hun- dred Biblical and archeological books and articles dealing with the creation myth of the Old Testament. Only a tiny selection of recent interpretations, only a small bunch of flowers (the comparison is perhaps suggested by the flowery language of some commentators) can be offered. Common to all modern explanations and exegeses is the basic concept that the tale of Eve's creation is a piece of Hebrew (or general Semitic) folk- lore and must be explored as such.

There seems to be a consensus among the experts that the saga shows Adam seeking in vain for companionship among the animals. The experience has, in Theodore Robinson's words,[11] "failed and Jehovah has recourse to a totally new method sending him into an anaesthetic sleep."

Biblical commentators compare the nature of this sleep to the divine sleep of Abraham, described in Genesis XV:12. "And when the sun was going down, a deep sleep fell upon Abraham, and, lo, a horror of great darkness fell upon him." The Lord promised Abraham and his seed a great future while he slept. The Hebrew word for this special kind of sleep is rendered in the Septuagint as *ecstasy,* in the Vulgate as *sopor.* The same term is applied to St. Peter's vision. We have already men- tioned the interpretation that Adam's sleep was designed to prevent him from observing God at work. Alan Richardson asserts[12] that behind this element of the parable there doubt- lessly lies the primitive notion that man must not behold the miracles of God which are secret processes known to God alone.

Almost all commentators agree that in his dream Adam saw God take a rib from his side and close the wound. Then he saw the woman and immediately, or "after a time the woman he had seen in his dream is brought unto him," he recognizes her.[13] Several commentators emphasize that no phrase comes near to being an equivalent of the Hebrew idiom Adam used to welcome Eve, virtually the cry, "That's it," or in Milton's words:

> "So absolute she seems—
> And in herself complete."
> (*Paradise Lost,* Bk. VIII, 547-548)

Hermann Gunkel has already pointed out that the Hebrew word for Adam's slumber is not the usual one used for sleep, but for "a deep, miraculous sleep of God" (I Sam. XXVI; Jes. XXIX:10; Job XI:23; XXXIII:15; Dan. VIII:10). Gunkel sees a deeper significance here: it is "a specially beautiful, very plastic feature. God's creation and work always remain a secret."[14] Why God took just a rib for his creative work is explained: "It had to be an inner part of Adam's body not very necessary, and he had enough ribs." Gunkel takes it for granted that the ancient Hebrew, when asked, would point exactly to the place from which the rib was taken.[15]

John Skinner explains[16] that the cause for the creation of woman was that no new creation "from the ground can provide a fit companion for man; from his own body, therefore, must his future associate be taken." For Skinner as well, Adam's sleep is a hypnotic trance intended to produce anaesthesia, "with perhaps the additional idea that the divine working cannot take place under human observation." Gerhard von Rade says quite similarly that the narrator wants to express the idea that "God's miraculous creation does not tolerate an observer."[17] God cannot be perceived acting; man can only worship God's work as already performed. In a recent book[18] Dietrich Bonhoeffer says that Adam did not really know Eve's creation had occurred: "But he knows that God had used himself, had taken part of his body while he slept. That Eve was taken from him is no cause for boasting, but for special thanks."

Edward Robertson found an original analogy in his interpretation of Eve's creation: "Perhaps at the back of the tale was the knowledge that in the plant world a cutting can be raised to reproduce the plant." That a rib was taken and not a limb may be due to the knowledge that the severing of a limb would leave him mutilated and permanently crippled.[19] To Paul Heinisch, professor at Nimwegen, the Genesis story means only that woman "is creature of the same nature and equal to man."[20] The Biblical writer has reason to emphasize this "because in antiquity woman was considered inferior to man and is still considered thus today with many people." The rib is near the heart—the Biblical writer wanted to say that man and woman belong together.

We conclude this brief survey of interpretations with these two concepts that are so flagrantly contradictory. There is, on one hand, a rationalistic concept in comparing the rib-operation with the process of plant reproduction. There is, on the other hand, the relapse into an allegorical, highly-idealistic and high-sounding explanation that sees the rib-operation as symbolic of the heart-to-heart relation between man and woman. Many attempts at interpretation of the rib tale deal with its problems in the wrong terms. It is, to use a gross exaggeration, like applying a band-aid to soothe a toothache.

Modern exegesis has without doubt made some valuable contribution to understanding the Biblical creation story. Yet it has not solved the problem of the significance of the Eve myth. It has only skirted it. Before the era of higher criticism and of modern exegesis, we groped in the dark in order to find an exit. Biblical scholars since then have guided us, but their explorations have led us to a point where we are now in a dead-end street.

Where do we go from here? We cannot accept the position that the myth of Eve's creation is only an indifferent piece of Hebrew folklore, a grotesque fairy-tale. Nor can we share the naive belief of fundamentalism which accepts the Genesis story as literally true.

CHAPTER IX

INTERMEZZO—OUT OF THE MOUTHS OF BABES

PROUD and delighted parents tell stories about the clever and wonderful sayings of their children. Their little boys and girls speak the most remarkable things. ("Children say the darndest things!"). My parents, alas, had very few occasions in which to brag about my precociousness. I was, it seems, a dreamy and perhaps even an indolent little boy. I have no memory of any such brilliant or amusing sentences, and, from what my relatives say, if there were any at all, they must have been few and far between. Yet there was a "bright saying" of mine I heard my father quote often and repeat to friends. I still remember the ill-concealed pride in his voice when he told it to an aunt of mine. I must still have been in elementary school when I spoke the odd sentence—but thereby hangs a tale about my grandfather on mother's side.

I had seen him many times during the summer vacations when we visited our grandparents who lived but a few hours train ride from Vienna. The picture of grandfather shows an old man with a short, pointed, white beard and a little cap on his head. He sometimes took a small silver box from his pocket to snuff tobacco. His name was Lazar Trebitsch and I was told much later that he was a well-known Talmudic scholar who had written some erudite treatises on Biblical subjects. When his wife died, he moved from the small community on the Austrio-Hungarian frontier where he had lived, to Vienna, and came to live with us in our rather small apartment.

I still remember the day of his arrival because one of his first actions both astonished and upset me greatly. There was a marble bust of a Greek god—was it Apollo or Zeus?—on the bookcase of our dining room. Soon after my grandfather arrived, he came out of his room, seized a chair which he clumsily climbed, and struck the nose of the Greek figure with a hammer. I can still visualize the mutilated head of the god and the ghostly impression it made on all of us children. Much later I understood what this then incomprehensible action meant. The old man was a zealous Jew and could not tolerate a bust in the apartment in which he lived. ("Thou shalt not make unto thee any graven image. . . .")

That act marked the beginning of a conflict between grandfather and father, which increased in bitterness and lasted many years: a fight interrupted only by short armistices during which the two men had amicable conversations. My father was a free-thinker. He disagreed completely with grandfather's opinions and would not stand for the intolerant attitude and bigotry of the despotic old man who insisted on having his own way. My poor mother, who shared my father's basic attitude, still felt very sorry for her old, lonely father. She tried to appease both excitable men, but in vain. In this conflict she was slowly destroyed, as though she were an object ground to powder between two millstones rotating in opposite directions. There was no common ground between a fanatic and an agnostic, between a medieval bigot and a modern mind. Later, I took my father's part and began to hate the old man whose tyranny had caused us so much grief. But at first I had been impressed by my grandfather as only a little boy can be by an energetic and forceful patriarch.

Shortly after he had moved into our apartment, he began to give me lessons in reading and writing Hebrew. I was soon able to read Hebrew (without vowel indications) which to my regret I have since unlearned. A few months later, I was allowed to attend the discussions my grandfather had with some Talmudic scholars. These were generally held in the evening after dinner. Several grey-bearded men with earlocks, dressed in old-fashioned and somewhat untidy kaftans, came to grandfather's room and were quickly involved in a vivid, and, what seemed to us children, a passionate debate about obscure passages of the Talmud. Admitted to this illustrious but bad-smelling circle of savants, I now assume, I sat silently in a corner of the room, utterly unable to follow the sophistic and hair-splitting arguments which were led according to a specific method of dialectics called *pilpul*.

During those disputations about the difficult problems of interpretation, the little boy often heard an expression which my grandfather explained to me when I asked about its meaning. The expression was *tomer verkehrt*. The first word is Yiddish and means "perhaps" or "maybe"; the second word is German and means "turned around" or "reversed." The expression was occasionally used in interpretation of difficult Bible passages in the sense that they should perhaps be reversed to be understood, or that their meaning might become clear should the text be read backwards. *Tomer verkehrt* was applied in a manner similar to our colloquialism, "Maybe the shoe is on the other foot." There were, no doubt, other technical terms for some logical rules and regulations as well as for sophistic tricks and turns. I do not know why the two words *tomer verkehrt* remained in the memory of the boy who was a silent listener.

During one of those evenings of theological debate the little incident occurred which my father sometimes related to his friends. My grandfather and his old students had been discuss-

ing at length the Genesis story of the creation of Eve, or rather
some of the Talmudic explanations of the Biblical narrative.
The grotesque Biblical tale they were confronted with must have
bewildered those old men as it had so many Christian and Jewish
theologians for the last two millennia. A long discussion about
the meaning of the Eve tradition had evolved according to the
procedure of the *pilpul,* but no solution of the problem had been
found. The meaning of the Biblical story remained obscure.

The old men sat there in silence and profound thought, mus-
ing over the enigma of the birth of Eve from Adam's side. It
was then that I suddenly burst forth. In the middle of the silence
I heard my voice say: *"Tomer verkehrt!"* I had the impression
that not I but someone else had spoken but, as soon as the
sound of the two words had died away, I was terrified. I had
not meant to say them. I had only been thinking aloud—expressing the idea that the meaning of the Biblical tale of Eve's
birth from Adam's side could be understood when one reversed
the main features of the story. Only much later did it dawn on
me that with those two words I had revealed that I knew the
secret of birth and delivery. As far as I can remember, no one
had yet told me the "facts of life."

My grandfather indignantly called my behavior impudence (he
used the Hebrew word "chuzpeh") and sent me out of the room.
I was never again allowed to attend the meetings of the Talmudists. It seems to me that on that day the seed of my subse-
quent fight for freedom of research was implanted in me.

I doubt whether that little incident would have left any
permanent impression on my memory had my father not smil-
ingly told it to some relatives in my presence. I must have
caught the tone of approval, even of pride, in his voice.

I was reminded of my childhood audacity almost twenty
years later when I first heard the psychoanalytic interpretation
of the Genesis saga of Eve's birth. As a little boy, I had an-

ticipated the discovery of the concealed meaning of the legend. I was therefore not astonished when I heard the interpretation, nor did I experience any feeling of satisfaction ("out of the mouth of babes . . ."). There was even a marked feeling of dissatisfaction with that concept because by then I had already gone far beyond that point.

CHAPTER X

THE PSYCHOANALYTIC INTERPRETATION

WHEN I first came to the Vienna Psychoanalytic Society as a guest in 1910, I met Hans Sachs and Otto Rank who had been members for several years before me. After I joined the Viennese circle, we became friends. In status and significance, both men represented older-brother figures for me. United in our admiration and love for Freud, stimulated by his ideas and enthusiastic about the new science of psychoanalysis, we were motivated by similar interests in research. We often spent our evenings together and discussed the research projects each of us hoped to accomplish. It was a beautiful and heroic time. Isolated but confident, we anticipated that we had a special role in the development of psychoanalysis. We were young and life was full of promise—"C'est jeune et ça ne sait pas."

I do not remember when Otto Rank, whom I admired, first told us—Sachs and myself—about his new concept of the creation myth. It was probably in 1912. I can still remember that it was late afternoon and we sat together in his studio in the Grünangergasse in Vienna. I was not surprised. I felt somehow that I had heard a similar interpretation a long, long time ago. Only a few hours later, on my way home, I remembered that once I, myself, had thought something quite similar and then the two words *Tomer verkehrt* and the scene in my grandfather's room came back to me. The vague sense of familiarity with Rank's interpretation was thus justified.

Prior to our conversation, Rank must have discussed his concept of the Eve saga with Freud because it is already mentioned in a letter Freud wrote to C. G. Jung, dated December 7, 1911.[1] In it Freud expressed his objections to exploiting mythological material at its face value in the service of psychoanalytic interpretation and uses the Genesis saga of Eve's birth as an example: "The creation of Eve has something about it that is quite peculiar and singular. Rank recently suggested to me that a reversal could easily have been brought about in the myth. That would make the tale clear. Eve would be the mother from whom Adam was born, and we should then encounter the mother-incest so familiar to us, the punishment of which and so on. . . ." According to this concept, the present form of the Eve saga is determined by a reversal of its original content. Freud maintains that "manifest forms of mythological themes cannot, without further investigation, be used for purposes of comparison with our psychoanalytic conclusions. One must first ascertain their latent original form by tracing them back through historical-comparative work to eliminate the distortions that have come about in the course of the development of the myth."

But Rank's interpretation was exactly the same one I had tentatively arrived at as a boy, and which I had expressed at that time in an unguarded moment. When Rank first developed his idea to Sachs and me, I was filled with admiration for him, as I had been on so many other occasions in which he showed his analytic brilliance and ingenuity of interpretation. When I first heard such concepts gleaned from many psychoanalytic experiences in his practice, it all seemed obvious—yes, even glaringly correct. Also, his explanation of the original meaning of the Eve myth was "nice and neat." Why was I, shortly afterwards, not satisfied with this highly original concept? Why was there the vague but definite feeling that Rank's interpretation did not solve the problem of the creation saga?

Soon after our meeting, other ideas about the Eve myth had occurred to me and I did not hesitate to communicate them to my two friends. These new notions had three features in common: they had been stimulated by Freud's book *Totem and Taboo,* were in a state of incubation, and were fully developed only much later. It does Rank credit that he mentioned them twice in his *Psychoanalytische Beiträge zur Mythenforschung* in spite of their immaturity and their unfinished form. It now seems to me that he considered them even more fully developed than they were and took projects whose blueprints I had discussed with him for definite plans of buildings. He wrote in that book that "Dr. Th. Reik. . . . will in a prepared work interpret another level of the Fall saga which will complete its original meaning in another direction" and that I would in the projected work "discuss the primal form of the myth and the elimination of the feminine element in the Genesis saga."[2] Those were my intentions, to be sure, but the book on the Fall myth was not published before 1956 and the essay I am presenting here shows that more than forty years have passed since Rank announced those interpretations as being imminent.[3] It is true, however, that at that time (back in 1912 and 1913), I had thought of my ideas only as a complement of Rank's interpretations of the Genesis myths. As time went on and years passed, my ideas took another direction. They were not only independent of Rank's views, but often in conflict with them as well.

During the years 1913 and 1914, some questions presented themselves to me which made me seriously doubt that Rank had found the answer to the creation problem. Was the riddle of that story solved simply by correcting the reversal brought about in the original tradition? And was that tradition, alive among the prehistoric Hebrew tribes, really as simple as to contain a statement that Adam was born of Eve and lived in incest with his mother? It seemed to me that the demonstration of the reversal mechanism did not explain, or rather did not exhaust, the meaning of the Eve saga. It only gave the framework of the early shape of the myth, nothing more. Several essential features of the Genesis account remained unexplained by Rank's interpretation.

It makes us understand the main part of the saga, namely the birth of Eve, but it conveniently fails to mention other features which do not fit into that framework As long as we are content to find the origin of the idea of Eve's creation from Adam's body, Rank's interpretation satisfies, or almost satisfies, our curiosity, but we immediately run into snags when we try to trace the other elements of the Genesis myth.

How, for instance, does the feature of the deep sleep fit into Rank's concept? Is it without significance that the Lord puts Adam—or in the psychoanalytic concept, Eve—into that deep sleep? We cannot conceive of it as a twilight sleep during delivery. That would be expecting too much from the traditions of half-primitive and half-nomadic tribes. Where is there a place for the rib operation in the analytic reversal concept? How can the fact be explained that God shaped Adam's body from this extracted part of Eve? Let us, for the sake of argument, accept the reversed tradition of the Eve-story as the primal, or as one of the primal, traditions: does not the story imply that Adam, and Eve, respectively were born as grown-up adult human beings? No tradition tells us about their growing up and becoming a man and a woman. The Biblical story of the Fall of the first couple immediately follows the grotesque narrative of Eve's creation. Adam and Eve appear from the first moment as a couple and Adam welcomes his mate with *Bräutigamsjubel* (the jubilation of a bridegroom), to use Hermann Gunkel's expression.

There is something wrong with that psychoanalytic interpretation or something—and something very essential—missing. Tracing the Genesis myth back to a tradition which, in reversal of the present saga, permits Adam to be born of Eve has, so to speak, provided us with a scaffold erected before the building of the house has begun. It presents the temporary structure for the purpose of holding the workmen and the material during the building. It certainly does not tell us anything about the form and the content of the construction as it will subsequently emerge.

Even when we attribute an important role to the mechanism of reversal in the formation of the legend, we do not know the reason for turning the content of the tradition around. What does it mean and why was it necessary? The mythological explanation sounds as if it were a parody of itself.

No, the myth of Eve's creation is not explained by the psychoanalytic interpretation. Let me, for a moment, return to our reaction to a medieval picture which presents the scene of Adam delivering Eve. We said that the impression this work of art gives is not that of a naive painting of the Biblical story by a religious artist. There is something bizarre or ludicrous in the picture. It is as if a grandiose mythological scene were accompanied by an ill-concealed grin.

We are tempted to compare the mysterious and mystifying story of Eve's creation with a rebus, especially with a picture puzzle. Was Adam not a gardener whom God placed in the Garden of Eden? Let us imagine such a picture puzzle showing a wonderful garden with trees, flowers and many animals, a paradise, very nicely painted. The caption asks, "Where is the gardener?"[4] The gardener is hidden somewhere in the picture, either in the branches of the trees or in the contours of the animals, in the clouds or in the outlines of the rivers. According to the rules of the game, he can be contained in the rebus standing on his head or in any other bizarre position.

The psychoanalytic interpretation solves the pictorial hide-and-seek by pointing out that Adam is to be found somewhere in the myth when the content of the myth is reversed, which means when the first male is born of woman. In other words, in our picture puzzle, we are advised to search for the gardener's spouse from whose body Adam was created. That gives us only a hint but does not reveal the woman's hiding place to us. Where is Eve concealed? We must explore the picture very carefully once more to find her. We must go in search of her. The analytic interpretation seems to advise us: *"Cherchez la femme!"* The query now becomes a quest.

CHAPTER XI

A NEW APPROACH IS NEEDED

THE REVERSAL of the roles of Adam and Eve in the interpretation Otto Rank gave to the Biblical creation story seemed at first to solve the problem posed by the Genesis narratives. To use a comparison: it demonstrated the trick performed as neatly as if we were shown a rabbit pulled from a top hat. Rank's interpretation was generally welcomed in psychoanalytic circles. We heard that Freud too saw in it the clue to the Eve saga. It was astonishing that just at that point I drifted away from Rank's concept, and the more surprising since I had arrived at the same basic notion as a boy. On the other hand, I could not agree with Jung's rather superficial interpretation of ancient myths.

Thoreau says: "If a man does not keep pace with his companions, perhaps it is because he hears a different drummer. Let him step to the music he hears, however measured, or far away." In my case, the music was indeed far away and in the strangest measure. It was produced by primitive rams' horns blown in early pre-Biblical times by nomadic tribes and later known as *shofars*.

My doubts about Rank's interpretation were originally vague but they became pretty solid a short time later when I became interested in the study of the initiation rites of savage tribes. Some months after I heard Rank present his interpretation of the Eve myth to us, Freud gave a lecture at the Vienna Psychoanalytic Society on the same subject which he had recently dealt

with in his new book *Totem and Taboo*. My study of the puberty
rites of the savages was conceived under the profound influence
of Freud's lectures and was presented to the Vienna Society two
years later in January 1915. But long before that, during my
study of the abundant anthropological material on the initiation
rites of African and Australian aborigines, an idea had occurred
to me which seemed to explain the Biblical Eve story and which
challenged the interpretation Rank had given.

The word "idea" is certainly too distinct and too dignified
a name for the hunch that first emerged and which slowly became sufficiently definite so that it could finally be verbalized.
I no longer remember when it first dawned on me that behind
the Biblical tale of Eve's creation was concealed the story of a
puberty rite followed by a union of the first mythical pair. I
trusted that initial hunch as little as the reader will who first
encounters it here. Those impressions seemed bizarre and were
soon rejected. Warned by so many examples I had read in books
of Biblical exegesis, I was unwilling to be lured and led astray
by some will-of-the-wisp analogies and similarities. Yet there
emerged certain clues in the study of the material beyond the
surface of the myth. They seemed to announce the presence of
some concealed figures and figurations. It was as though slight
movements behind a curtain began to reveal secret happenings;
a hidden sequence of events seemed to form a vague pattern.

When I came upon the idea of an analogy between the Genesis
story of Eve's creation and certain features of the puberty initiations recorded by anthropologists and missionaries, I did not
think too much of it, nor about it. I did not pursue the thought,
but the thought began to pursue me. An idea, once admitted
and given hospitality in your brain, cannot easily and casually
be dismissed: it soon assumes an independent life of its own.

With the re-emergence of the idea, a certain suspense is felt
—an almost tangible expectation and a challenge to follow it
and to see where it leads you, in spite of its irrationality. It is
very possible to compare such an idea, once it is formulated

and internally verbalized, with a voice which refuses to be silenced. Well, that voice seemed to talk nonsense. What could the myth of Eve's creation from Adam's rib have to do with the alleged initiation festivals of prehistoric Semitic tribes? Yet the outline of such a subterranean thought connection emerged more and more clearly and became irresistible.

In that train of thought, psychoanalysis was not really used as a method of investigation. It became rather a new approach to a problem which could not be solved by any other means. An intuitive grasp of similar features seemed to reveal this still undiscovered significance within the Biblical myth. I studied the commentaries and the other material again and after a grand detour of forty odd years returned to the problems of initiation into puberty—hopefully equipped now with better instruments to meet the unconquered problem.

It cannot and should not be denied that in the realm of arch-aeological psychoanalysis (as I have called the branch of analytic research dealing with reconstruction of prehistoric myths, cus-toms and history[2]) imagination also has its place beside the exact logical deductions drawn from the scarce materials at our dis-posal. Yet, a shot in the dark, if directed by an informed guess, can sometimes hit the target.

When Professor Werner von Heisenberg of Göttingen,[3] one of the eminent physicists of our time, once heard that a young student of his had turned away from theoretical physics to write novels, he said: "Well . . . his imagination was perhaps sufficient for that." Just as imagination is needed in the field of atomic physics, so it is necessary in the realm of psychoanalytic recon-struction to penetrate the vast darkness of prehistoric times.

Perhaps I did not lack the imagination necessary to grasp the hidden threads running from the Genesis story to the remote realm of primitive initiation ritual, nor the persistence to follow them when they seemed to be lost in the secondary overgrowth and overlay of material. I had learned from Freud, with whom I had enjoyed so many wonderful conversations, not to deny or run away from difficulties emerging from the exploration of complex psychological material. I had absorbed his habit of not disavowing basic convictions one had obtained after long self-criticism. Freud had taught us, his Viennese students, to face the difficulties, contradictions and inconsistencies that could often be explained subsequently and sometimes even turned into corroborating evidence. One had only to proceed, sincerely and self-critically, to a justifiable conclusion. The habits of thought and the direction of exploration I had absorbed from Freud, the attitude toward one's own initial resistance, served me well. Yet, alas, I had not absorbed his splendid moral courage as well.

I had enough independence of thought to follow my idea about the significance of the Eve myth and even to express my disagreement with Rank's accepted explanation, but with this my intellectual energy came to an end. I did not, as I had planned to do, write a book about the secret meaning of the Genesis story. After having jotted down a provisional draft, I shelved the research project and turned my interest to other problems in psychoanalysis. I am not able to state how much of this "giving up" was a "giving in," a yielding to Otto Rank, whom I considered my intellectual superior and who then held the place of an older brother. The effect, however, was that my hypothesis was submerged when Rank published his interpretation of the Biblical myth in his *Incestmotiv* and in his *Psychoanalytische Beiträge zur Mythenforschung*. It might be fairer to say that my interpretation lived a shadow existence similar to that of Adam in rabbinic legends, where he appears as a long, formless, colossal and lifeless being before Yahweh breathes into his nostrils.

Forty-eight years have passed since I first stated my interpretation of the Eve myth to Rank and then to Freud. This long interval of waiting and maturing has done no harm to the presentation of my thesis, although it has deprived it of much of the youthful vivacity and spontaneity it once had. In this presentation I have tried to follow the example of my great teacher, although I am painfully aware of how far it lags behind the

method of his pioneer-work. I recall now the manner in which
he sometimes began a lecture at our Psychoanalytic Society in
Vienna (when he presented a case of neurosis or a new theoretical assumption). He occasionally started the lecture with a statement that sounded utterly incredible or paradoxical. The
audience was clearly incredulous. Everybody listening asked
himself, "How is that possible?" or thought, "That cannot be!"
This method of Freud's is unforgotten and unforgettable to every
student who had the privilege of attending those lectures. How
few of us are still alive! He followed the analytic material
step-by-step and analyzed the significance of the details that
brought him to a conclusion which finally became irrefutable
and irresistible. The listener was left with the conviction not only
that it could have happened in the manner Freud delineated but
that it could not have happened in any other way. The following
chapters attempt to follow Freud's method of presentation.

I introduce the second part of this book with a surprising
statement: the Genesis narrative does not present the story of
Eve's birth, but a distorted tradition of Adam's rebirth.

At this point, we are not only turning a page but are also
leaving for a time the whole area of Biblical myth. With determination, we focus our attention on a series of phenomena which
geographically and temporally are very remote from the field of
the Yahwistic narrative. In due course we shall return, we hope,
better prepared to solve the problem of Eve's creation.

PART TWO

THE SOLUTION

And till thine this deepest behest:
Die to win thy being
Art thou but a sullen guest
Upon earth unseeing

GOETHE
July 31, 1814

CHAPTER XII

THE GREAT TRIBAL MYSTERY

SEVERAL TIMES during the last sixty years sociologists and anthropologists, as well as historians, have pointed out that puberty rites have a special significance for the evolution of society and of civilization. Heinrich Schurtz declared, in 1902, that the initiation festivals are the most important event in primitive societies and of longer duration than birth and marriage ceremonies.[1] J. G. Frazer stated that the initiation rites are the "central mystery of primitive society."[2] Building on the foundation of these and many other anthropological researches, and especially on Freud's *Totem and Taboo*,[3] I tried to show (in 1915) the psychoanalytic meaning of those rites for the religious development and the social organization of savage tribes.[4] After an interval of almost fifty years, I picked up the threads of those earlier trains of thought when I attempted to present the biblical narrative of the Exodus and of the Sinai revelation as a distorted account of initiation of the Hebrews.[5] Almost simultaneously, Mirca Eliade showed the religious meaning of initiation and its far-reaching effects in societies from primitive tribes to modern civilization.[6]

In spite of these and other careful and explicit books and monographs on initiation rites in ancient civilizations and among primitive peoples of our time, the impact and significance of those rites are far from being properly understood and evaluated. Why is that? There are certainly reasons quite apart from the almost proverbial reluctance of scholars to accept new ideas that shake the foundations of traditional notions. One of the main reasons for the lack of understanding is to be found in the very nature of the subject itself. Those rites are inviolably secret, which means that outsiders—women and uninitiated members of the tribe, as well as missionaries and anthropologists—are excluded from them and cannot get any information about even unimportant details of the rites. On the other hand, the novices, initiated into the tribal mysteries, must solemnly vow not to divulge anything of the contents, forms and functions of the initiation rites.

Almost all experts agree that the puberty rites, as we found them in different forms in preliterate societies, contain the germ and the pattern from which the ancient mysteries of the Egyptians and Greeks subsequently evolved. Those "rites de passage," to use van Gennep's expression, were also at the core of the various secret societies, so widely spread amongst savage and half-civilized people in Australia, Africa and America.[7]

There is a body of ritual and teaching which is supposed to bring about a decisive change in the status and attitude of the novices. In those "rites de passage," a boy is separated from his mother and passes through a series of ordeals that take him from childhood and bring him to adulthood. He becomes a responsible member of his tribe. The initiation marks the end of a period of life and the beginning of a new phase, a *vita nuova*. The highlights of the mystery—if the paradoxical expression is permissible—are the rites of "death and resurrection," as Frazer and other anthropologists call the drama, or as it is otherwise named, of "death and rebirth." Characterization of the rites makes us see that there is no contradiction between those two descriptions. For the primitive mentality, initiatory death provides the clean slate on which will be written the successive revelations whose end is the formation of a new man.[8] Mirca Eliade, whose recent book deals with the religious meaning of initiation, points to the primitive belief that a state of being cannot be changed unless the previous form of existence is first annihilated. Therefore, death in the initiation is indispensable for beginning a new life. It is remarkable, however, that in many primitive tribes the symbol of this initiatory death is darkness or night, sometimes the belly of a monster or even of a womb.

In spite of the great variety of rites in different civilizations, the basic features of all initiations are much alike. Anthropologists have recently emphasized the social and psychological aims of the initiation rites which present striking similarities. B. Malinowski[9] describes these common features: ". . . the novices have to undergo a more or less protected period of seclusion and preparation. Then comes initiation proper, in which the youth, passing through a series of ordeals, is finally submitted to an act of bodily mutilation: at the mildest, a slight incision or the knocking out of a tooth; or, more severe, circumcision; or, really cruel and dangerous, an operation such as the subincision practiced in some Australian tribes. The ordeal is usually associated with the idea of the death and rebirth of the initiated one, which is sometimes enacted in a mimetic performance." The second and more important part of the initiation is the protracted instruction of the novices in the sacred myths and mysteries of the tribe and the unveiling of certain sacred objects by the elders of the tribe.

The first phase of the initiation ceremonies is the segregation of the novices from their mothers and from all women. They are brought into the bush or into a separate camp where they are to be instructed in the tradition and lore of the tribe. According to the experts, all the performances and gestures during the operations are "only the repetition of exemplary models,"[10] which means repetition of events that took place in mythical time or in the "dream time," as the Australian aborigines call it. In the performance of the initiation ceremonies, the history of the mythical ancestors is reproduced and renewed.

The initiate is, as he himself and all present realize, "no longer himself; he is the great 'dream time' hero whose role he is re-enacting, even if only for a few minutes."[11]

The separation of the novices from their mothers is often performed in dramatic scenes; sometimes the novices are simply "stolen from the mother."[12] The boys are led into the sacred ground from which women and children are excluded. Among the Australian Kurnai, they lie on their backs, covered with rugs. They are supposed to see and hear nothing and fall asleep. A Kurnai headman said to A. W. Howitt: "If a woman were to see these things, or hear what we tell the boys, I would kill her."[13]

Separation from the mothers means a rupture or sometimes a violent break with the world of childhood. The mothers are convinced that their sons will be killed and eaten by some divine monster or god. But the novices who were intimidated and terrified also believe that they will be killed. According to a myth, reported by R. G. Matthews,[14] the god Daramulun of the Australian Wiradjuri tribes kills the boys, cuts them to pieces, burns them and restores them to life as "new beings, but each with a tooth missing." In many tribes a dramatic mock performance of killing the novices takes place; in other tribes they are put to sleep. The initiatory death and rebirth complement each other in the puberty rites. In other words, the resurrection of the novices corresponds to a new birth. As a matter of fact, the novices in the Brahmanic initiation in ancient India were called the "twice born."[15] In Buddhist imagery the second birth is likened to that of the chick by breaking the egg shell. The same image can be found among the Kavirondo Bantu who speak this sentence to the initiates: "The white chick is now creeping out of the egg, we are like newly fired pots."[16]

With the Tabim tribe in New Guinea, the initiation of young men takes place at intervals of several years. The most conspicuous part of the rites consists in circumcision, performed in the seclusion of the forest. Women are told that the novices are swallowed by a monster called Balum who vomits them up again and in doing this, bites or scratches them and thus inflicts the wound of circumcision. After several months of seclusion, the young men return to the village where they behave as if they were newborn babies. This is "why the young circumcised Papuans march back to their village with closed eyes; this is why, when bidden to sit down, they remain standing stiffly, as if they understood neither the command or the action."[17] The Ceram boys admitted to the Kakian society totter in their walk when they return to their home and "enter the house backward, as if they had forgotten how to walk properly. . . . If a plate of food is given to them, they hold it upside down. They remain dumb, indicating their wants by signs only. . . . Their sponsors have to teach them all the common acts of life, as if they were newborn children."[18]

Instead of being circumcised, the young men of many tribes are otherwise mutilated; for instance, teeth are knocked out, hairs are pulled out, lips or ears are perforated. It is of great significance that the novices, immediately after initiation or new birth, as we can now say, are given a new name. This widespread custom is found not only among the tribes of south-eastern Australia, but also among very primitive people; for instance, the Yamana and the Halakwulup of Tierra del Fuego.[19] In most tribes of Africa, Oceania and North America, forgetting the past after initiation goes so far that the novices recognize neither their families nor their friends and have even forgotten their previous names. Among some tribes of the Kuta of the Kyoye (Ndassa) the novice is severely beaten, which is supposed to "kill" his old name so that he may be given another.[20]

In most preliterate societies, a male individual thus has two names, one before and another after initiation. We can easily understand the bestowal of a new name when we remember that with it a new person emerges, the name being an immanent part of the man. The newborn novice has to have, of course, a different name.

Among the Arunta, Kaitish and Vumatjera tribes every individual has two names—a personal name, frequently used, and a second, secret one. Among the Waramunga tribes, the sacred name is given only to a fully initiated man.[21]

Among many primitive tribes, the end of the initiation is marked by sexual license. Among the Amayosa tribe as well as among the Zulu Basutos, the circumcised youth may possess any mature girl. Some Autralian tribes believe that the initiated men must have sexual intercourse after the rites or they will die. Such beliefs are, of course, not general, but at all events the initiated young men are allowed to marry. A. Barton is of the opinion[22] that circumcision amongst the Semites was at first performed upon the male at the time of marriage and several Biblical passages, for instance Gen. XXXIV:22, seem to confirm this view. The Arabic word "hatuma," like the Hebrew "chosan," bring circumcision into intimate connection with wedding and marriage. According to C. M. Doughty,[23] some Arabs do not circumcise the boy, but when he reaches the age to take a wife, the operation is performed in the presence of the maid he intends to marry.

The above description of the puberty rites is not much more than a sketch. It is focused upon certain features of the initiation and leaves other equally or even more important aspects of these festivals unmentioned. The religious meaning, the initiation of the young men into tribal customs and myths, the special characteristics of rites with various tribes and their development into initiation into the secret societies are not considered here. I can give only two reasons for this apparently arbitrary presentation. Those neglected sides of the puberty rites were fully discussed and their significance demonstrated in three previous books of mine.[24] Another presentation would amount to repetition of what was said there.

Secondly, such a delineation would be inappropriate here. I wish to compare certain features of the Genesis story of Eve's creation with some traits of the puberty initiation, reconstruct the original, and the much-distorted, oral tradition of the Eve saga among the Semitic tribes from which the Hebrew version evolved. For the purpose intended, it would not only be superfluous, but also confusing, to present a complete picture of the puberty rites of savage and half-savage tribes. A sketch will suffice since those rites are used here as material for comparison —only as bricks for the building to be constructed, or rather to be reconstructed. It is in the nature of a sketch that only certain features are put forward while others are neglected or left out. Justice Felix Frankfurter said of a lawyer that he treats all facts as if they were born equal. In avoiding the mistake of attributing the same significance to all aspects of the primitive puberty rites, we have selected only some features which are relevant to our comparison.

CHAPTER XIII

NEW CLUES

AFTER the grand detour, we are led back to our starting point: the concealed meaning of the Biblical Eve story. My hunch was that behind the account of the creation of Eve a distorted tale of Adam's initiation is concealed. This would mean that the Genesis story contains characteristic features of an old oral tradition focussed on a puberty initiation of the first man. It seems to me that these features are still palpable under the surface.

We have already decided that we would not deal here with every aspect of the primitive puberty rites and we cannot expect to find them again in an unaltered form in a late myth.

But before we proceed, we should remind ourselves of the fact that the primitive tribes to whose rites we referred are on a much older and evolutionally lower level than the rites from which the Hebrew people evolved. We assumed that the forgotten oral tradition we are trying to reconstruct is to be dated back to the time before the immigration of the Habiru into Canaan—that means at least thirty-five hundred years ago. Even then those nomadic invaders were not desert barbarians with a low culture. They had been subjected to the influences of Mesopotamian and Egyptian civilization. The old tradition of the Hebrew tribes, already changed, was then subjected to further and far-reaching alterations with the introduction of Yahwism and in the religious and social innovations of Moses.

Our situation is similar to that of an anthropologist who tries to reconstruct the original tradition of Australian aborigines who not only had their own long tribal development, but were, for several centuries, exposed to the religious and social influences of the British colonial system. The reconstruction will necessarily have only an "iffy" character and, therefore, cannot hope to claim complete authenticity.

The second difficulty we are confronted with lies in the very nature of the material at our disposal, the secrecy with which all important parts of the initiation were shrouded. The deep impression that the rites must be carefully guarded from women and children is intensified by the pledge of silence which every initiate has to take. The secrecy with which the puberty rites were enveloped was continued by the societies of half-civilized tribes and was handed down to their heirs in the mysteries of ancient people. These tendencies in the older generations are responsible for distortions of the original tradition and their effects can still be felt in the late Biblical account of Eve's creation, which appears as a mystery. Traces of that concealment are still perceptible in the veiled language in which the Biblical narrative is expressed. Celsus observed that Jews as well as Christians consider the account of Eve's creation from Adam's rib a mysterious allegory.[1] There is even an allusion to the Genesis passage in the epistle to the Ephesians, whose author says of it: "This is a great mystery." (V-32)

After this fair warning and preliminary remarks, we return once again to our subject. We consider the saga of Eve's creation as part of an original tradition of the Habiru tribes, handed down from generation to generation. Other fragments of that heritage have to be reassembled and put into their places. In that very old oral tradition, the secret lore of the tribes was transmitted to the adolescent boys during their initiation. It is not instruction in the modern sense, but presentation of the tribal myths, the story of supernatural beings and of mythical ancestors—of how the world was created and what happened then.

Tales originally loose and unconnected were much later tied together in the form of longer epics. It is the presentation, originally in dramatic performances of events that took place "at the beginning of time."[2] At the center of those tales is the life of the mythical ancestors, of what they did and what happened to them.

If we compare these elementary "biographies" of the tribal ancestors in the myths of Australian aborigines with the oral traditions later embodied in the Genesis stories, we arrive at an outline of a biography of Adam and Eve. The Supreme Being created them, a male and a female, from the dust of the ground. (The tales of the Paradise and the other of the Original Sin belong to another "cycle" and were joined much later with the creation story.) When Adam grew up the Lord caused a deep sleep to fall upon him. At this point our new interpretation begins, founded on the comparative material of anthropology and history. After having reached puberty, the first human being undergoes initiatory death. Where is the basis for such an assumption? It is in the sentence: "And the Lord God caused a deep sleep to fall upon Adam, and he slept."

The Hebrew word used for "sleep" makes it certain that it was not the usual kind, but a miraculous, divine sleep, a kind of trance or ecstasy. The commentaries pointed to several Biblical passages in which that expression is used in this particular sense, Job speaks of it (IV:13-17) when he says that secrets were unveiled to him "from the visions of the night, when deep sleep falleth on men. Fear came upon me, and trembling, which made all my bones to shake. Then a spirit passed before my face; the hair of my flesh stood up." Daniel tell us that he was in a deep sleep "on my face, and my face turned toward the ground" when he felt a hand touch him and he heard a voice (X:9). In those states of deep sleep or trance, intense feelings of fear and fright are experienced. These emotions come to clear expression in the powerful description of the panic experienced by Abraham before the Lord made a covenant with him: "And when the sun was going down, a deep sleep fell upon Abraham, and lo, an horror of great darkness fell upon him."

Adam's deep sleep is of the same kind. There is no doubt that it is akin to death or is a substitute for it, a death-like experience. (Compare "To die, to sleep. . . ." in Hamlet's soliloquy, or Prospero's "Our little life is rounded with a sleep.") The comparisons of the poets only continue the Biblical conceptions in which death appears as a kind of sleep, for instance, "Behold, thou shalt sleep with thy fathers . . ." (Deut. XXX:16).

We now compare Adam's situation with that of the boys of primitive tribes before their initiation. Neglecting for the moment the fact that Adam is conceived as the first man, as a being with no navel strings attached, we consider him as an adolescent boy separated in an enclosure. It is conceivable that in the original tradition Eden was such a prepared "sacred ground," an isolated camp like those in which the Australian boys live during their initiation, and was transformed by a later myth into the Paradise of the Biblical narrative.

The general supposition of almost all primitive puberty rites is that the adolescents are killed by gods or demons and after some weeks or months they are reborn as adults and members of the tribe. Not only the women and children believe that this initiatory death is a fate awaiting all boys, but the novices themselves are convinced of it and are very frightened. During the seclusion period, the priests or some masked men often perform pantomimic acts imitating the slaughter of the novices. In many tribes the initiation took place in such a way that the boys were put into deep sleep or into a trance-like state by the medicine man. The story of the death of the boys, of their dismemberment by a god, and eventual restoration to life as "new beings, but each with a tooth missing," is then told to the women and children, a ritual which can be seen in the Wiradjuri tribes.[3] Other versions of the story have the monster or god who kills the boys perform another operation—for instance, circumcision. The

Adam myth presents a telescopic view of this initiatory death ritual: the Lord puts the primeval ancestor into deep sleep during which a rib is taken from his body.

The removal of the rib embodies another part of our circumstantial evidence. This clue still belongs to the ritual of death and rebirth which we traced in the puberty ceremonials of preliterate people. When a young man is initiated into the Ndembo society in Africa, he allegedly drops dead. He will be dressed as a dead man and carried out of the village. His body supposedly decays except for a single bone. After some months, the priest takes this bone and effects the resurrection of each young man. The resemblance between this mystical bone procedure and the Adam myth is obvious.

The Siberian shamans maintain that they "die" in their initiation and lie inanimate for some days in a solitary place.[4] During this time, they are cut to pieces by demons or by their ancestors' spirits. Their bones are cleaned, the flesh scraped off and the eyes torn from their sockets. Their bones are then covered with new flesh and in some cases they are given new blood. The pattern of dismemberment is found almost everywhere. The master of the Araucanian shamans makes believe that he exchanges the novice's eyes and tongue for others and puts a stick through his abdomen. The candidate for the Kuksu society among the River Patwin is supposed to have his navel pierced; he dies and is resuscitated by a shaman. At Malekula the novice is supposed to be cut to pieces by the master. The pieces are joined together again when the master puts the youth's arms, feet and head back into place. Among the Dyaks of North Borneo the novice's head is supposedly cut off, his brain removed and washed, to give him a clearer mind. Also in some initiations of Australian medicine men, cutting up the body and exchange of viscera are essential rites.

Mirca Eliade,[5] from whom I am borrowing these examples, remarks that the initiatory dismemberments of the novices deserves a long comparative investigation. They are disconcerting and have not yet been explained. The scholarly author points out that they resemble the myth and ritual of Osiris, without, conspicuously enough, mentioning their resemblance to the Biblical Adam narrative. Yet this resemblance is obvious, beginning with the death-like sleep and the removal of a part of the body, and ending with a new life. In the primitive myths, it is a demon or mysterious totem god who performs the operation. In the Bible, it is Yahweh, the creator of heaven and earth. Yet the deity, who has risen so high, cannot deny his descent from a barbaric night-demon.

We would not be embarrassed if we were asked to demonstrate a transition from the strange rites of savage tribes to the religions of Europe. Here is an instance from the legends of a highly developed form of religion. Amina, the mother of Mohammed, gave the son she had just born to a Bedouin woman, Malima. As is well known,[6] this woman took the boy into the desert with her, fed him and brought him up. Legend reports that Malima became so frightened by a terrifying event that she decided to return her foster son to his mother. Once, when Mohammed and his brothers led the cattle to pasture as usual, two men dressed in white suddenly appeared, took him and threw him to the ground. They opened his breast, removed a big lump of black blood, washed the place and cleaned the heart, closed the opening and disappeared. The resemblance of those two men, who functioned as messengers of God, to the mystical ghosts who attack boys in the Autralian bush and open their bodies to substitute new organs for their lungs or hearts, is clear enough.

Before we discuss the interpretation of the rib operation in the Biblical tale, a sidelong glance will be sufficient to remind the reader of the meaning given to the Genesis passage by the commentators. Some of them freely admit that the choice of the rib is puzzling. Others, like Alan Richardson,[7] see in it a "wonderful allegory": a woman's place is at the side of the man and she ought to be the sharer in all his life. The explanation that the manner of Eve's creation from Adam's rib "was such as to indicate that only when like is joined to like is the union indissoluble"[8] is in a similar vein. Thorlief Borman asserts that the choice of the rib must have had a profound meaning for the Biblical narrator and points to a Greenland myth in which woman is created from the man's thumb.[9] He adds that the thumb is "the strongest, most valuable and wonderful part of all limbs." The rib was, at all events, chosen because of its inherent meaning, not because of its usefulness as production material, "because the building of a human body from a rib is inconceivable."

A better understanding of the rib episode can be arrived at when the operation is conceived as a replacement for another mutilation. Edward Stucken expressed the view that the removal of the rib presents the remnant of an older myth of castration.[10] He connects this notion with a similar feature from Greek mythology: woman originates from Adam's rib as the love goddess, Aphrodite, from the cut-off phallus of Kronos. Otto Rank picked up the thread of this interpretation later and followed it further.[11]

There are two clearly distinct parts of the myth, although they seem to be intimately connected: the rib operation and the fashioning of the woman. To avoid the danger of confusion, we consider it advantageous to make a sharp division between them. The removal of a part of the body and the use of this part as production material for something or someone else are acts originally independent of each other. If this assumption is correct, it would be justifiable to treat the two features in our interpretation separately and only later try to find an explanation for their joint appearance in the Adam myth.

We turn first to the rib operation, to the removal of Adam's bone—to the skeleton in the closet of the Lord. The other day a politician advised: "Keep many balls in the air and people just don't notice the misses." Such an attitude might well be proper in politics, but it is not compatible with the spirit of research. In this area, hits and misses are equally noticeable. Honesty demands the admission that we have not yet succeeded in solving the problem of Adam's rib operation.

CHAPTER XIV

ADAM'S CIRCUMCISION

SOME RABBIS explained that Adam, as well as some patriarchs, were born already circumcised. It is easy enough to recognize in such a statement the embarrassment the rabbis felt when they had to admit that circumcision of Adam is mentioned nowhere in the Bible. It can be better understood when we hear the Talmudists declare that Adam and Eve were born as twenty-year-old man and woman.[1] We know that many preliterate people have the custom of dating the age of their young men from the time of their puberty initiation, as if their boys were born then, when they are supposedly "newborn."

Returning to the discussion of the rib operation in the Biblical tale, we are reminded that in many countries, instead of being circumcised, the novices are mutilated in some other manner. These injuries are substitutes for circumcision and sub-incisions of the penis, and are recognized as such by the majority of anthropologists. Since all operations on the male body are unconsciously conceived as castration, Stucken and, following him, Rank, are correct in interpreting the rib operation as a remnant of an emasculation, especially when we add that circumcision, psychoanalytically seen, presents a mitigated form of castration.

In many primitive tribes, there is the belief that the young men whom demons or tribal gods deprive of some organs receive other and better ones in their initiation. This feature is doubtlessly the result of a later development of the puberty rites, since we do not find such notions in the savage tribes of

Australia. Among the Bukaua and the Tami, the lads are supposedly swallowed by a ferocious monster called Balum who
vomits them up again. In spewing them out of his maw, he bites
or scratches them and circumcision is interpreted as the wound
thus inflicted.

In the analysis of the representative case of a five-year-old
boy, Freud could show that ideas of a similar kind are to be
recognized in the thoughts and fears of children. At first Little
Hans was afraid that a horse would bite off his penis. Later
he thought the plumber would take the penis away and replace
the small genitals with bigger ones like those of his father.[2]

Setting the result of our interpretation into its proper place
now, we arrive at the following interpretation of the Biblical
tale: when Adam reached the age of young manhood, the Lord
isolated him, put him into a lethargic trance and circumcised
him at the end of the seclusion. The continuation of the tale
which reports that He "closed up the flesh instead thereof"
simply describes the healing of the circumcision wound.

The following verse, "And the rib, which the Lord God had
taken from man, made He a woman and brought her unto the
man" is truly puzzling and disconcerting. It is also the part of
the saga most difficult to explain and the inner core of the
mystery. As has been mentioned, the passage contradicts the
account of the first Genesis chapter according to which God
created man male and female together. When we now try to
translate that story into the terms of the primitive puberty rites,
we are confronted with an even greater problem: nowhere in the
initiation do we encounter such a transformation. In the puberty
ceremonies, as well as in the rituals of admission into primitive
secret societies, some organ of the young novices is allegedly removed from their bodies and in a mystical way replaced by a
better or more "spiritual" one. A change of such a radical kind
as the transformation of this organ into a woman is nowhere to
be found in the ideas of preliterate people. There are two ways
to deal with the problem confronting us. We can dissect it,

discuss the multiplicity of possible interpretations and so come to grips with it; or we can dodge it, proceed as before, and struggle with it subsequently when we can restate it in new terms, or when we are better prepared for the quest or its meaning.

We will not be swerved from our determination to pursue the comparison of the Biblical tale with the puberty rites and will simply march along the road we have chosen. After we have seen where it leads us, we can always return to this point. For the present, then, we neglect this passage and continue as if the account had told us that after Adam's recovery the woman was brought to him. Then follows the union with her.

Thus conceived, the sequence of the Biblical tale tallies well with the outline of the puberty rite; initiatory death, circumcision, marriage. We know that after the healing of the circumcision wound the novice is considered a full member of the tribe and is allowed to marry. The reader is here reminded of the intimate connection of the Arabic and Hebrew expression for "circumcise" and "bridegroom" and of the allusion to this link in thoughts appearing in the cry of Moses' wife, Zipporah, "Thou art a bloody husband to me." (Ex. IV:26)

Of course, the expression "marriage" is chosen here because we conceive of the situation in Eden as seen from the viewpoint of a late tradition. It would, perhaps, be preferable to point to the relationship between sexual intercourse and circumcision. In some primitive tribes, intercourse is obligatory after circumcision. A Ceramese boy must have intercourse with some girl immediately after circumcision—it does not matter with whom—by way "of curing the wound." Boys, as well as girls, of some central African tribes must have intercourse as soon as possible after their initiation otherwise, according to their belief, they would die.[3]

We will return to the discussion of that part of the tradition in which the rib operation is intricately related to the conjugal bond between Adam and Eve. For the moment we set the debate aside

in order to bring to a close the comparison of the Genesis tale
with the initiation rite.

The last link between the two phenomena which have nothing
in common on the surface is based on the factor of a new name
for the initiated. We learned that the novice of preliterate people
received a new name on his admission into the world of adults.
This is thoroughly logical and consistent since he is no longer
his old self, which is dead, but is quite literally newborn, a baby,
just come into the world. A name must therefore be bestowed
on him. When W. Koppers attended the ceremony of initiation
of the Yamana of Tierra del Fuego, he was given a new name to
indicate that he was reborn into that primitive tribe.⁴ Among
some Juta tribes, the novice is severely beaten, which is said to
"kill" his old name so that he may be given another.⁵ With the
beginning of a new life after the rebirth, the new member of the
tribe or the secret society is given another name, since the individual's name is equivalent to his true existence.

But where is there any analogous trait in the biblical creation-
story? The first human being has his name, Adam, and there is
no other new name. Adam is no proper name. The Hebrew word
is a common noun denoting a human being. The etymology is
uncertain. "Adam" has been connected with the Assyrian word
"adum" ("child," or "one made" or "created") and with the
Hebrew root "ȧm" which means red and can be interpreted as
alluding to a reddish color of the skin. Any connection with
Adapa, the hero of a Babylonian myth, is very unlikely. The
Genesis passage in which Yahweh-Elohim is presented as forming man (*Adham*) of the dust of the ground (*Adhamah*) is, of
course, a word-play and cannot be taken as a scientific derivation. Yet there might, in this alleged derivation, be a trace of an
old myth in which the first man was created by an earth goddess.
If we take the psychoanalytic interpretation of a reversal in the
tradition seriously, the primal ancestor could have introduced
himself to his mother with the old palindrome: "Madam, I'm
Adam."

But where is a change of name of our common ancestor indicated in the scripture? The immediate and obvious answer is: "Nowhere." Yet, such a change can be concluded with great probability. That is to say the Biblical tale of Adam contains enough circumstantial evidence from which a change of name can be inferred. Adam means human being (in Latin *homo* as distinguished from *vir* "man"). When Eve emerges, Adam welcomes her (Gen. II:23) and says: "She shall be called Woman because she was taken out of Man." Here, of course, is a wordplay again, a derivation quite similar to that of Adam from *Adamah* or *homo* from *humus* in Latin. The Hebrew word for woman, employed in the passage, is *issa,* distinguished from *is,* which is man. Some scholars have pointed out[6] that English is fortunate in being able to reproduce this assonance of wo-man and man, while other languages are driven to "tours de force"; for instance, *virago* and *vir* in Latin (Männin in Luther's translation).

In giving the name woman (*issa*) to the new creature, our primal ancestor calls himself by a new name: *is* (man). Not Adam any longer, but man. That means a grown-up male who has acquired all the privileges and rights of an adult after his initiation and circumcision.

It seems to me that here we have more than a clue. When we consider the many distortions and alterations to which the oral tradition was submitted, we are inclined to see in this passage an indirect proof of a change of name from Adam to man. The evidence, here adduced, is, though internal, quite tangible.

After having rounded off our comparison, we must take up again the challenge presented in the Biblical junction of Adam's rib operation and the appearance of the first woman. We can now return to this problem with a clear conscience since we are convinced that we have discovered some basic and significant analogies between the myth of Adam and the puberty rites. Some features of an early tradition from which the Biblical account originated came to the surface in our analytic reconstruction—

in spite of all secrecy and distortion. Some traits, such as Adam's deep sleep, the rib operation, the union with a woman and the new name, must now be understood as survivals of that old and suppressed tradition. Like small pieces of a hard, frozen material, these parts remained somehow intact while other peripheral parts were carried away by the wave of the new social and religious movements.

Together with so many scholars, we were puzzled by the Biblical narrative according to which woman was created from Adam's rib. This tradition was so tenacious that in medieval language woman was often spoken of as "the rib." What an odd expression! But how much more fantastic and fanciful is the process itself, by which a woman is formed from a man's rib! Yet there cannot be any doubt: the meaning of the Biblical text is not ambiguous. This passage is so central that its inclusion in the comparison between the Adam myth and the initiation rites would be fatal to our hypothesis if we could not put it into its context. The building we erected threatens to collapse.

Yet, the house seemed to have been built on such solid ground! How many puzzling features of the creation story became comprehensible by comparison with the puberty rites! Adam's deep sleep, the operation of the rib, the birth that appeared as a new birth of the initiated, the union with a sexual partner, the changed name of the youth who has become a man. All the features seemed to fall into place. And all in vain?

At this impasse, we must remember that the oral tradition from which the myth evolved had been submitted to many and decisive alterations. Is it not possible that the Biblical version presents an already much distorted, a much modified and falsified story? The work we are doing is comparable to that of an archeologist who tries to dig up a prehistoric sanctuary beneath the remnants of an early Christian church. We must not forget that the construction we ventured to undertake is a reconstruction.

We are painfully aware of the fact that what we are doing is patch-work and piece-work, as unfinished as all scientific research in prehistory. The Talmud says: "It is up to us to do the work: it is not up to us to complete it."

Another train of thought might prove even more helpful: it concerns the similarity of myth and dream—a psychological kinship so often demonstrated by psychoanalysts. The point I want to make here is the following: dreams as well as primitive myths show an impressive amount of condensation of the material they try to present. Both are restricted in expressing certain things adequately because of the scarcity of means at their disposal. The dream, for instance, can express logical relations between dream thoughts only indirectly or through displacement. In a dream, it might go thus: "Because this is so, therefore I must behave in this way." Strictly speaking, the dream has no means by which to express those logical relations which we indicate by using terms like "because," "although," "if" and so on. It can express a causal connection between two parts in no other way than by sequence—by letting one part be followed by the second.

Another kind of presentation of such a causal relation is that a person or a thing in the dream content is transformed into another. One element succeeds the other in the dream—that often means "either" but sometimes simply means "because." The primitive myth finds itself in a similar emergency situation. It also has only poor ability to express logical relations. Yet, dreams as well as primitive myths are eager to appear coherent and intelligible. We know that this appearance of coherent and logical unity is due to secondary elaboration that works behind the scenes of dream productions and that this effort is more or less successful, especially if helped by small additions and displacements when the dreamer tells us his dream.

If we now make use of these insights into the psychology of dreams and myths in re-examining and rearranging the passage reporting that Yahweh made a woman from the rib he had taken from Adam, can we make sense of this nonsense? Is there a method in this madness when we take those peculiarities of myth

production into account? Let us see what we have previously
learned about the life of primal man. In our interpretation we
find only a sequence of events: Adam is circumcised (the rib
operation) the emergence of the woman, his spouse, then follows. In primitive initiation rites there appears another but not
dissimilar sequence according to reports from various preliterate
people: after the puberty operation (circumcision, subincision,
extracting teeth, and so on) the novice can marry; or rather,
he cannot marry until he is circumcised. In other words, a man
becomes suitable for marriage, or acceptable to a woman as
husband, only after he has undergone that operation. This also
seems to be the meaning of that obscure Exodus passage in which
Zipporah protects Moses from Yahweh's wrath by saying, "Thou
art a bloody husband to me."

Circumcision then became the condition of marriage or of
legal sexual intercourse. Myth can present the logical relation of
limitation or restriction which we express in the words "on the
condition that" only in the form of one fact succeeded by another. Only after Adam was circumcised could he obtain a
spouse. The rib 'operation which we recognized as a substitute
for circumcision is the middle term between Adam's old and new
state.

Primitive myths as well as dreams depict relations of this kind
by the only means at their disposal: they assert that one person
or thing is transformed into another. In this awkward or elementary manner of presentation, the rib in the Biblical story is
changed into a woman, thus tying the condition of circumcision
to sexual union. This mode of myth-making so similar to that of
dream production, is also determined by the secondary elaboration which manufactured the appearance of a coherent whole in
order to make the original meaning of the primitive myth un-
recognizable.

So far, we have a general outline. But there must have been
special conditions facilitating the alleged transformation of a
rib into a woman. There are and, remarkably enough, these con-

ditions are even more intimately connected with the puberty
rites. In the Biblical narrative the Lord God made the rib, taken
from man, into a woman. Something no less miraculous is supposed to happen to the novices during their initiation. There is
also a mysterious transformation but it takes place on the body of
the candidate. The bones or the skeleton play the same role in
the puberty rite as the rib in the Genesis story: they are the material from which a new person or a new life is made. In the
initiations of the shamans and in many southeastern Australian
tribes, the Supreme Being or his representative, the medicine
man, resuscitates the novice, who allegedly has long ago died,
by reviving his bones or his skeleton. Among the Ammasilik
Eskimos the apprentice falls dead at a certain moment and remains lifeless for three days and nights. A gigantic polar bear
devours all his flesh and reduces him to a skeleton; revived, the
apprentice becomes a shaman. Similar views are held by the
Indo-Tibetans and Mongolians. The essence of such post-mor-
tem experiences is defined by Mirca Eliade who describes the
ritual as based on a very ancient religious idea belonging to the
hunter culture: "Bone symbolizes the final root of animal life,
the mold from which the flesh continually arises. It is from bone
that men and animals are reborn. After their life is reduced to
the essence concentrated in the skeleton or some bone 'they are
revivified'; that is, the skeleton is brought to life by being given
new flesh."[7]

The frequent references to bones in the Old Testament (Job.
IV:4, Jer. XXIII:9, Ps. XXXV:10) indicates the definite notion
of their inherent vitality and even of consciousness diffusing
through them and the whole body. The life that is supposed to
be still inherent in them can be renewed by anointing them with
blood.[8] Ezekiels' famous vision (XXXVII:1-10) originates in
this concept: the Lord set the prophet down in a valley which
was full of dry bones. "And he said unto me, son of man, can
these bones live? . . . and as I prophesied, there was a noise,
and behold a shaking, and the bones came together, bone to

bone. . . . the breath came into them, and they lived, and stood upon their feet, an exceeding great army." Here we encounter the same idea of resurrection from bones that is a prevalent feature of the initiation rites and whose outline we sensed in the Biblical Adam myth. The transference of the concept of rebirth of the primal ancestor from a bone or rib to the creation of Eve seems obvious. It is determined by the sequence of initiation and marriage. The secondary and artificial connection between the two tales is established by Adam's sentence: "This is now bone of my bones. . . ."

We found a logical connection between the rib operation and the emergence of Eve: the first event is the condition of the second. Only after Adam was circumcised could he obtain a wife. For Adam, Eve is "bone of my bones, and flesh of my flesh" in the same sense as Moses is for Zipporah a "bloody husband." This means acquired only through circumcision.

Some biblical scholars, like Hermann Gunkel[9] and before him Karl Budde,[10] have pointed out that the Paradise story, as told by the Yahwist, has two threads: one is the creation account and the other the narrative of the forbidden fruit. Both stories were artificially joined together subsequently. Those two stories are different and originally had nothing to do with each other. Gunkel assumes that the production of the woman really belonged to the creation story. In spite of our appreciation of the ingenuity of the commentators who succeeded in separating the two heterogeneous materials, we cannot agree with their assigning the Eve story to the creation tradition. Gunkel is certainly correct in his assumption that the two stories attracted each other until they became fused because they both deal with the primordial age of mankind. Yet the Eve story is a continuation of Adam's biography: in veiled language it tells us of his initiation and circumcision and of his finding a spouse.

We arrived at a reconstruction that permits us to attribute Eve's appearance to the concealed thread of an initiation tradition. We recognized vestiges of such a tradition in certain clues and no longer doubt that this concealed story was woven into the creation tale in order to mislead and deceive the uninitiated. The account fitted into its surrounding so perfectly that they functioned as protective camouflage.

The connection between the rib operation and Eve's appearance in the Biblical narrative is also meaningful. Stripped to the bone, as you can well say in this case, Genesis relates a simple story of what happened to our first ancestor after circumcision: first boy meets first girl.

CHAPTER XV

THERE'S THE RUB

HAVE WE solved the puzzle of Eve's creation? Sober self-criticism will tell us that we have only focused on a specific aspect of it; namely, on the relation between the rib operation and the emergence of Adam's help meet or spouse. The myth of the birth of Eve appeared to be a distorted and displaced tale of Adam's rebirth, followed by union with a woman. The fusion of the two ideas was facilitated by the affinity of the notions of rebirth and birth.

This resemblance and the reciprocal attraction of the two circles of ideas explains much. But it does not explain everything. After having first guessed and then recognized the furtive movements behind the smoke screen of later elaboration, the secret of the puberty rites became visible and the Genesis story revealed to us its hidden meaning. When we now compare notes with the commentators of this part of the Holy Scripture, we get the impression that we have not read the same book.

When someone once asked Einstein how he came to discover his relativity theory, he replied, "By challenging an axiom." The small discovery in the field of archeological psychoanalysis upon which we have stumbled has also been obtained only after challenging the axiom of Bible exegesis that the Genesis story presents the birth of Eve. Before our decisive finding everything seemed to be centered on the creation of woman and was understood in this sense. We listened to many voices and somewhere heard another melody in the great symphony of primordial time.

It was as if we recognized a familiar tune in the elaborations and variations, a motif we had once heard elsewhere in the puberty initiation of savage and half-civilized people.

We then found a new frame of reference in which the myth of Eve could be lodged. Here, too, is a process of birth, but in the form of a rebirth. Put into its proper place that part of the Genesis saga relates the biography of our common ancestor, a story with a beginning, a middle and an end. Adam's birth, his growing into manhood, his initiation and circumcision, his marriage, that unpleasantness in the Garden of Eden, the children of the couple, and death. Yet it should not be forgotten that those tales were originally independent of each other and that they were very much later integrated into an integrated whole. The Genesis story is thus a collection of traditions put into a specific literary frame. This is done in the traditional technique of early Semitic literary works and is similar to that used in the famous Babylonian Gilgamesh epic.

We have undertaken a lonely job of research and our study in depth has led to the insight that the Biblical story does not tell of the creation of woman but of the recreation of man, or the reaching of manhood of the primeval hero who became united with a woman.

Yet precisely at this point a new question arises. It vexes us and will not allow itself to be shelved. How did that interpretation or, if you like, misinterpretation of the story as a birth from Adam's body evolve? It is not to be found in the commentaries of the early rabbis. They conceived of the rib operation as the beginning of a new creation, but in the sense that the rib became the material from which the Lord manufactured the woman. Only much later, strictly speaking in the time of the Gnostics, did the concept become widespread that Adam gave birth to Eve as a woman gives birth to the child—the "great mystery" to which St. Paul alludes. (Ephes. V:32). From here it is admittedly a long way to the depiction in many medieval pictures where Eve is portrayed emerging from the body of sleeping Adam. But the strange concept of this kind of birth from Adam's side only advances a notion which had been there long before in a germinal state.

The problem would seem simpler if we could assert that the concept is a late allegorical or symbolical interpretation introduced into an old tradition distorting and radically changing it. But there's the rub. In many initiation ceremonials we find the rebirth presented as a real birth. A part of the initiation ceremony gives the impression that the father or his substitute really gives birth to the boy. The rebirth allegedly takes place and is by no means spiritual. Even the Christian ceremony of baptism cannot deny its origins lie in those pagan initiation rituals and even in that Christian spiritual rebirth, the candidates are reborn through the male Saviour.

This second birth, conceived as a rebirth in the flesh, is the most mysterious rite of many Australian and African tribes. It is, for instance, universal among all clans of the Kikuyu. The rebirth was originally combined with circumcision, but when there was trouble, "the old men settled the matter by separating the two."[1] From the great variety of the puberty rituals in which rebirth is acted out as a form of childbirth, a few examples should be mentioned. In the west of Ceram, one of the Indonesian Islands, the boys to be admitted to the Kakian society are at first blindfolded. They are conducted into an oblong wooden shed situated under the darkest tree in the depth of the forest.[2] When a boy disappears in this gloomy hut, which presents the womb to which he returns and from which he is to be reborn, a strange scene takes place: a dull chopping noise is heard; a fearful cry rings out; and a sword or spear, dripping with blood, is thrust through the roof of the shed. This is meant to demonstrate that the boy's head has been cut off. He is carried away by the devil. "At the sight of the bloody sword, the mothers weep and wail, crying that the devil has murdered their children." The lads staying in the Kakian house are warned by the chief, under pain of death, "never to reveal what has passed." After some days the men who acted as the boy's sponsors or guardians return with the glad tidings that the lads are restored to life. The ritual imitates the act of childbirth and the boys, returning to the village, behave as if they were babies, as if they were "born yesterday."

The Liberian Poro society also has a ritual in which the boy admitted undergoes an initiatory death. The crocodile spirit swallows him and keeps him in its belly a long time. He is scarred by the mark of the Poro made by the spirit's teeth. The crocodile spirit, after swallowing the boy, is "in a state of pregnancy" until the close of the initiation when those of the boys "who are still alive" are "born" by him.[3] Here again we find rebirth by a male spirit. Among Australian tribes the rebirth of the initiated boys is acted out; men carry them on their shoulders as women carry babies. They even perform the same purifying rituals as women do after childbirth. During the incision the male sponsors in New Guinea hold the boys on their back and generally behave as mothers consoling their babies. Some authors, for instance Bruno Bettelheim[4] and Margaret Mead,[5] state that during the initiation rituals men try to take over the functions of women, especially that of childbearing.

When we return to the theme of Eve's birth from Adam's rib, where are we? It seems we have found a new clue. But that is not enough. Clues must be interpreted. Their significance must be clarified. Hasn't this long detour brought us back to Rank's interpretation that the concealed meaning of the Eve saga can be found by undoing the reversal which operated in the development of the myth? Eve was not born from Adam's body but Adam from Eve's. It seems as if we have returned to a point we had already passed; yet it is not the same point.

The analogy with the ritual of initiation has led to the concept that the myth of Adam giving birth to a child has striking resemblances to a certain part of those rites in which the fathers pretend that they bring the boys into the world. At the same time we recognize the sharp differences between the notions in the myth and the initiation rites. In the puberty rites the generation of older men, the fathers, are supposed to bring forth their sons. In the Eve saga a man gives birth to a female who is at the same time his spouse.

Let us continue, however, to move in the direction we have followed until now. Some commentators assure us that Eve is originally the figure of a goddess; we can now add, of the great mother goddess of the ancient Orient. As such she would correspond to the divine mother whom the Babylonians called Ishtar, the Egyptians Isis, the Phrygians Cybele, the Greeks Aphrodite, and the Romans Venus. This goddess awakened desire and love and was the object of sexual impulses and of awe. In most forms of the myth of the mother-goddess, a lover of hers appears, a son-god called Adonis, or Attis, Osiris, or Tammuz. If we now put Eve (or perhaps originally Adamah, the earth-goddess) into the place of this divine goddess of fertility and sexuality, we arrive at the statement: Eve (or Adamah) has brought Adam into the world. He then became her lover. Besides this reconstruction, another one is indicated: Yahweh, a father-god, produced Adam. The original form of the saga must have had the form: Adam was born as the product of sexual intercourse between a father-god and a mother-goddess.

The emphasis of that myth is, of course, on his birth from the great goddess whose lover he became as Tammuz, Osiris, Attis, or Adonis, and who enjoyed, alas, for too short a time, the favor of the deity. The reversal of the birth can have no other meaning than to deny the origin of Adam. It is a determined negation of the fact that Adam was the son of the goddess whose husband he became. This refusal to acknowledge the mother-son relation has the obvious meaning of denying the incestuous nature of Adam and Eve affiliation.

The myth formation in which Adam gives birth to Eve is, therefore, the end product of a process by which his descent from a mother-goddess is most energetically denied. The mythical saga of a reversal of the roles of the sexes stands side-by-side with the other Biblical account in which the Lord formed Adam from the dust of the earth. It is difficult for us to decide which of the two accounts is the older, but we are inclined to assume that the reversal tradition is a secondary modification of an earlier one.

What advantage do we derive from the comparison of this Eve tradition with the corresponding part of the initiation rituals? First: we see the saga of Eve's creation no longer as an odd piece of fantasy, but in the context of other, more familiar, primitive beliefs and notions. Second: we understand that Rank's interpretation of a reversal is inadequate, because it oversimplifies the origin and development of the myth. When we now consider that part of Adam's story, the other features (the deep sleep, the rib operation, the welcome of Eve) fall into place. Third: we become keenly aware of the distinct difference between the Biblical myth and the special rites of the initiation in which a rebirth of the candidates takes place. In the primitive rites, the men of the tribe (the father generation) bring forth the boys. In the Biblical narrative, Adam, whom we now consider as a representative of a son-figure, gives birth to a woman.

There is, superficially, another difference: in the rites of the savage tribes, the boys are supposed to be newly born and their behavior that of babies. In the Biblical myth, Eve is born as an adult woman; yes, even as a bride. We understand, of course, that the ritual supposition that the initiated boys are newborn babies is a pretense. As a matter of fact, the boys have at least reached the age of puberty and in many cases that of mature manhood, when they can marry and have all the other rights of tribesman.

In the Genesis saga, Eve really appears as a grown-up female. At this moment, we are reminded of Michelangelo's fresco in which Eve emerges from the body of sleeping Adam, but it is clear that his is a telescopic presentation. We also remember the opinions of those rabbis who declared that Adam and Eve were born as twenty-year-old people. We translate, of course, "were reborn, became initiated members of the Hebrew tribe."

The nature of the Eve myth cannot be understood until we recognize what is meant by the alleged, and often dramatically presented, birth of the novices of savage tribes from the bodies of older men. Their behavior cannot be explained as utter nonsense, silliness or clownish toomfoolery; in this madness there must also be some meaning.

I remember vividly a lecture which the New York psychoanalyst Dr. Dorian Feigenbaum gave as a guest of the Vienna Psychoanalytic Society. It must have been before 1925. Dr. Feigenbaum discussed the word salad of the schizophrenics and similar verbal symptoms and showed their psychological determinants. In the ensuing discussion, Freud remarked that it was very difficult to produce purposely absolute nonsense. Even the silliest things manufactured consciously revealed some sense if psychoanalytically interpreted. Freud added that while it was not possible to produce intentionally utter foolishness, quite a few books by German scholars are full of effortless and unintended nonsense.

Our next step is to understand the meaning of those grotesque portions of the puberty rites and to use the insight gained in the solution of the Eve problem. In our search, we remain aware that in general myths evolve from rites. Our return to the discussion of initiation rites is legitimate since myths appear to be of only secondary value if compared with the rites.[6]

CHAPTER XVI

A HOAX IN THE STONE AGE

PERHAPS the intellectual challenge confronting us could be met more easily if the special myth of Eve's creation were compared with similar sagas in the mythology of other peoples. It is not accidental that the meaning of the word "comprehend" ("com" and "prehendere" in Latin) is dual: to understand and to include. The significance of an event or configuration can often be quickly recognized when similar phenomena are compared with it. But did we not assert that the Biblical tale of Eve's creation shows a singular character? That is so, but this is restricted to the one feature that Adam's creature also becomes his mistress.

All the other traits of the Biblical narrative are by no means unique and parallels can be found in the religion and mythology of many people of antiquity. The sagas of Greenland, in which the first woman was created from the thumb of a god; the myth of Karh of the Yuracarr, who produced a son for himself from a torn-off toenail;[1] Dionysius sprang from the thigh of Zeus; Daksus from the toe of Brahma; Pallas Athene was the daughter of Zeus from whose head she leapt in full armor—all these are illustrative.

Instances like those mentioned, and others which could have been added, show that the mythical concept of a man (or a male god) giving birth to a son (or a daughter) contains nothing strange for the various people of antiquity. According to the Babylonian priest Berossus the god Bel cut off his own head and men were fashioned out of his blood. In Vedic myth, man springs from the blood of the slain Purusa; in Greek myth from that of the slain Titan.

Let us now cast a backward glance at the rituals of the savage tribes who were the ancestors of those ancient people with higher religions and more advanced mythological concepts. As reenacted in festivals we are unable to discover essential differences in their myths of man's creation. The only divergence seems to be that the suggested birth in the puberty and initiation rites concerns only sons while in Greek mythology, a god (for example, Zeus) brings forth a daughter.

In the case of the myth of Eve's creation, we note with astonishment that the strange nature of her birth was accepted without much comment by most theologians of the older school. Very few of them compare this myth with those of other people and almost no theologian gives much thought to analogies or similarities of this kind. In a recent article of the London *Punch* C. S. Lewis comments that religious people are not "interested in religion." He says, "Men who have gods worship those gods; it is the spectators who describe this as 'religion'. . . . The moment a man seriously accepts a deity, his interest in 'religion' is at an end. He's got something else to think about."

Even the Biblical scholars did not pay much attention to Eve's being made from the rib of Adam—but when they did, they offered rational, so to speak antiseptic, explanations. The anthropologists and ethnologists, as well as the researchers in mythology, are of course very interested in the varieties of religious experience. In their explorations, they took the ancient and primitive mythologies into consideration and compared them with the Eve myth. Their investigations, as in J. G. Frazer's *Folklore in the Old Testament*[2] for instance, were very informative in producing a wealth of comparative material. Yet none of them, it seems to me, penetrated to the core of the Biblical saga.

The first breakthrough can be credited to Otto Rank, whose interpretation of the reversal of the sexual roles marks the prog-

ress made in the psychoanalytic explanation of the Biblical creation myth. As far as I know, neither he nor any psychologist
or ethnologist has brought to our attention the fact that there
are subterranean connections between the Eve story and the
secret initiation ritual, and that relics of a prehistoric time of savage rites are preserved in the myth.

After we have recognized the meaning of those initiation
rituals, preserved like fossils in the Old Testament narrative of
man's creation we can hope to discover "the story behind the
story." The explorers, of course, have different opinions about
the meanings of the puberty ceremonies, but they all agree about
one aspect of them. The rituals themselves speak in clear and
unambiguous language here. From the separation of the boys
—one can almost call it their kidnapping[3]—to the pretense that
they are to be killed or eaten, together with the severe prohibi-
tions and intimidation of the candidates, the purpose is clearly to
frighten and terrify the women and the uninitiated of the tribe.
The effects of those rites, from which we may infer their motives,
is the following: the mothers of the boys cry and wail and mourn
for their sons who are to be killed. The women, terrified by the
bullroarers whose voices they interpret as those of the monster
called Balum, "look on from a distance, weeping and howling,
for they are taught to believe that the lads, their sons and
brothers, are about to be swallowed up. . . . How then, can the
poor women be sure that they will ever see their dear ones
again?"[4] There is an abundance of similar description about this
part of the ritual among the tribes of Australia and Africa.

An Australian native, asked about the significance of the
puberty rites, gave the following surprising answer: "We eat the
pigs and lie to the women." He meant, of course, the pigs prepared for the Balum ghost who will release the boys from his
belly only if he receives a sufficient number of roast pigs. Other
details of the initiation tally well with the information given by
that Australian native: the boys were shown the bullroarers and
taught how to swing them, and at the same time threatened with

death if they betrayed to the women the secret that the noises were not those made by ghosts. It is the same with other sacred tribal objects and with part of the tribal lore.[5] In the initiation rites of the Indians in the Chaco, and also among the tribes in Tierra del Fuego, boys are prepared for their future responsibilities by listening to the old men who teach them the tribal lore. At the initiation they learn that the spirits they had greatly feared as children are only masked men. The spirit impersonators perform dances near the camp in order to terrify the women.

What then is the place of the supposed rebirth of the sons from the older men in the ensemble of initiation rites? Some of the anthropologists, Bruno Bettelheim to name one, have given the explanation that "one of the purposes of male initiation rites may be to assert that men, too, can bear children." The implication is that there is a competition in which men pretend that they can do as well as women in this area. It has sometimes been emphasized that men are envious of woman's ability to bear children.

As I have pointed out in my book *The Ritual* almost forty years ago one of the most important purposes of the puberty rites is to loosen the tie between boys and their mothers and to bind the novices to the society of men. This part of primitive education, marking the growth of boys into maturity, is accomplished by drastic means. The strongest tie binding the child to the mother is, of course, the fact that she gave birth to him and his dependence resulting from that. To break it, the male child is supposed to die, to be killed and to be born by man again, by his father or a father-representative. This new or newborn being begins a fresh existence as an adult and as a member of his tribe. His rebirth—at least on the low levels of primitive society—is not meant symbolically at all, but is really and plastically presented in a mimetic performance. The road from this rebirth to baptism and confirmation, to death and resurrection in Christ, is indeed a long one but it moves in a straight line.

It is essential to recognize this most significant feature of the

initiation and its purpose of breaking the tie between boys and
their mothers by pretending that the initiated are born again by
men. That rebirth is significant in undoing birth from a mother.
Considered from this viewpoint, the dynamics of reversal in the
Eve myth appear in a new light. It is as if the men of the tribe
announced that they now gave birth to their sons, who from that
point on belong to them and no longer to their mothers and
sisters—a method of education meant to drag adolescents from
the women to the camp of men.

Let us now try to fit the rebirth feature into the whole context
of the puberty rites. Let us furthermore consider the silence and
secrecy with which they are surrounded, their intentions and their
effects on women and the uninitiated. In the fictions of the death
and resurrection of the boys, the deception of women and the
tricks played upon them, and the whole succession of untruths
and pranks, we cannot fail to recognize the nature of this aspect
of initiation. During the initiation of the Kwoma of New Guinea,
a carved head representing a powerful spirit is shown to the
novices. They are told that this "is a hoax . . . but that the secret
must be carefully guarded from the women and children."[6]

No doubt, the ritual of rebirth is a hoax and its position within
the initiation ceremonials marks it as the zenith of a performance whose whole purpose is to deceive the uninitiated.

The Eve myth, with which we compared the rebirth part of
the initiation, is a hoax and the Biblical story of Eve's birth is
the hoax of the millennia. What is a hoax? According to a recent
definition[7] it is "a deliberately concocted untruth made to
masquerade as truth." We are profoundly astonished at the fact
that this mischievous quality of the Genesis-saga was so rarely
recognized by the Biblical scholars who tried to explain the tale
of Eve's creation from Adam's body.

We think of the long sequence of scholarly interpretations of
the Eve saga—explanations, many of which are either abstruse
and fantastic, or rationalistic and abstract—and we wonder at
the longevity of hoaxes. Scholars in the past have neglected con-

spicuous signs of the nature of this hoax, signs which were as broad as the church doors on which Eve's figure is sometimes carved as emerging from Adam's body.

There is, no doubt, a serious side of the rude joke that must have delighted the tribesmen who were pretending that the novices were reborn in the puberty initiation. There must also be motives in the Hebrew tradition which lead to this formation of the Eve saga. We would like to know what the psychological meaning of the mystification is.

CHAPTER XVII

ABSURDITY AND MOCKERY
IN THE EVE MYTH

THOUGH we recognized Otto Rank's interpretation of the Eve myth as brilliant and original, his explanation of reversal evoked justified criticism in two directions: Rank's hypothesis does not explain how his suggested original version fits into the context of the Adam story. His reversed story is, in a sense, suspended in mid-air. Why should the birth of Adam be told again after it was narrated in the previous Biblical account? The second argument to be advanced is equally problematical, at least without further explanations: What would the motives or the reasons be for the reversal of the myth that Rank assumes?

Looked at naively, the Biblical narrative is utterly incredible. Shakespeare says:

> If this were played upon a stage now,
> I could condemn it as an improbable fiction.

Let us for a moment imagine that we have to look at the scenario of the Eve story from a theatrical point of view, from a seat, as it were, in the stalls. There are three *dramatis personae* or, strictly speaking, only two, since Yahweh is invisible. These two persons, Adam and Eve, have made themselves known to us briefly. When the curtain rises, we see only Adam, sunk in a long, deep sleep. If this were a play, and we were sitting in the stalls, we might feel inclined to complain of the lack of action, but what follows, the birth of Eve from Adam's body, is truly dramatic. It leaves no doubt about the character of the play. It is a farce.

There must have been strong emotional or mental reasons for transforming the original myth metamorphosing the birth of Adam from a mother-goddess into the Biblical story in which the birth process appears to be reversed and as such, contrary to nature and absurd.

Unlike quite a few Biblical scholars, we have faced the narrative of Eve's creation and declared that it is a deliberately concocted nonsensical story, which means it is a hoax of the Hebrew tradition, a deception manufactured and imposed upon the uninitiated. The thesis presented here may seem paradoxical, but the history of science is to a great extent the history of paradoxes that have become commonplace. ("Sometimes a paradox, but now the time gives it proof," to quote the Danish Prince.)

We were interested in finding the sense in the non-sense. The comparison of the Eve myth with part of the puberty rites gave us the first and the most valuable clues. They made us understand that the reversal of sex roles in the birth story originated in the wish of the father generation to make the boys believe that they are reborn from men. In the sequence of rebirth and of the appearance of woman, a high degree of condensation of the saga material is achieved: there is circumcision (presented as a rib operation in the Bible), rebirth and the sexual union after the healing of the wound, and the novice's return to his community.

The logical connection between circumcision and marriage cannot be expressed by the myth in any other way than via the mixed formation in which the operation is identified with finding a mate. The identification of rebirth with Eve's appearance is presented in Eve's birth itself, a transition facilitated by the notion of birth and new arrival.

The element of reversal is difficult to explain and can be brought closer to our understanding by analogy with the production of dreams. The dream expresses contradiction or objection, saying "no" in a special, one might almost say witty, form. Instead of saying, "No, on the contrary," the dream turns a specific piece of its content around. The relation of the conflict existing between two parts of the dream material is expressed by their reversal. Since the dream cannot express logical relations otherwise, it presents the thought "on the contrary" by behaving unreasonably or perversely like "Mary, Mary, quite contrary."

Myths, at least in their primitive forms, show a similar mode of presentation. Instead of saying, "Adam was not born from Adamah or any other mother-figure," the myth denies this descent by turning the statement around and presents Adam giving birth to a woman, to Eve. We know the source of this contradiction, or objection lies in acknowledging birth from a mother, from a woman. This piece of the myth material originates in that ritual of the initiation where the birth of the boy from his mother is denied and replaced by a "rebirth" from a man. But at this point the myth conspicuously goes beyond the pretense of the puberty rites. It reverses the sex roles, lets Adam or the adolescent male give birth to a girl. This element needs special psychological evaluation.

Here again comparison with the dream mechanism is helpful. Perhaps it is best to illustrate my point by presenting a simple instance of a dream interpretation I have mentioned elsewhere.[1] A young woman dreams that she sees her husband in jail with chains on his arms and legs. He holds their baby in his arms. The residues from the day before, or the materials from which the dream is formed, are the following: the evening before her husband had made some remarks about the hard work men must do and the easy tasks women have at home. The visual picture of the dream presents the continuation of thoughts his wife had before falling asleep. They might be translated into the language of conscious thinking as follows: "I wish you were in my situation, bound hand and foot, imprisoned at home and having to take care of the baby all day." The dream mocks the husband, makes fun of his view about the easy kind of work his wife has as compared with his.

The opinion, "That's nonsense," or "That's absurd," is expressed in the dream by presenting a grotesque or absurd situation. When criticism, sarcasm or a sneering attitude are in the dreamer's mind, the dream production presents something absurd or ridiculous. It changes a part of the latent dream content into manifest form. The absurdity of the dream should not express a simple, "No," but together with the objection to the husband's statement, a tendency to mock or laugh at him. Instead of saying, "That's foolish" or "ridiculous," the dream contains a silly or ludicrous element. Hamlet behaves in a similar manner when playing the fool with Polonius and the courtiers. The motif of a *reductio ad absurdum* is found in many folktales and *märchen*.[2] There is, for instance, the typical story (well known in German, Baltic and Spanish folklore) of the man whose foal strayed into a field with two oxen belonging to a neighbor. When he went to bring home his foal, the neighbor claimed it. The case was taken to the king who awarded the foal to the man who swore it belonged to his two oxen. The next day a man was seen fishing in the road with a huge fish net. The king went out to question him. It was the rightful owner of the foal, who said, "As easy to catch fish on dry land as for two oxen to produce a foal."

The problem of absurdity in the myth of Eve's creation can be solved with the help of the analytic insights we gained from Freud's method of dream interpretation. The myth, in its formation and in mockery goes beyond the point reached in the puberty rites and comes to expressing biting sarcasm. In their hoax on the mothers the Australian tribesmen said: "We, too, can bring children into the world. The boys are reborn from us and will, from now on, belong to us, to men's society." The Biblical myth goes much further in its mockery. It ridicules the mother's claim by demonstrating its absurdity. The Eve story seems to say: "We men can give birth too, we can even give birth to female children."

In presenting this ludicrous assertion, the myth sneers at the mothers who want to keep their children for themselves on the undeniable grounds that they gave birth to the boys.

The last part of our interpretation must deal with the appearance of coherence or logical consequence in the Biblical narrative of the Eve creation. Superficially, the Genesis account seems to have a correct connection with the preceding and the following parts of the tale. It does not contradict the premise and is in accordance with the Lord's statement, "It is not good that the man should be alone. I will make him a help meet for him."

This appearance of coherence and cohesiveness—once you have accepted the miraculous as natural—is produced by a secondary elaboration. Again the comparison of myth and dream production is helpful here: a psychic factor operating in or after the dream endeavors to give it an orderly and intelligible look in the mind of the dreamer who later remembers it. It is obvious that this apparent coherence is not achieved in all parts of the myth. The agency attempting to perform the synthesis is not always successful so that in spite of the attempt at secondary elaboration some pieces, such as the transformation of the rib into Eve, seem confused or muddled.

Every investigator secretly hopes he will find the clue to end all clues and make the deductions to end all deductions and thus arrive at a complete solution of a puzzling problem. Every investigator must realize that he is far from achieving such a complete and ideal understanding, and must be content with achieving some partial solutions. There will always be odds and ends he must leave on the scene of his exploration. We can only hope that this pioneer attempt at interpretation has unearthed threads not recognized by previous investigators.

Before we bring the interpretation of the Eve myth to a close, it is appropriate to point once more to the fact that the

tale of Eve's birth has many similarities with the myths of other
ancient peoples and of many preliterate tribes in our own time.
The birth of Pallas Athene who sprang fully grown from
Jupiter's forehead is only the most famous example of myths
of this kind. In several other myths, a male god or supreme
being gives birth to a female figure. We would assume that this,
or a similar motif, appears when the myth development of a
people has reached a certain evolutional point. It is impossible
for us to determine what point this is.

Another problem is of interest to the historian of religions
as well as to the anthropologist and psychologist: is there a
basic difference between those myths in which a woman is born
from a god and the Biblical narrative? In trying to answer this
question we neglect, of course, divergencies of minor importance, such as variations determined by the cultural levels of
the people, alterations and distortions of the traditions by later
religious or social influences, and so on.

There is, it seems to me, at least one basic difference. In
those other myths, the female creature born from a cult hero,
an ancestor or a god is and remains his daughter. From Adam's
side there emerges a woman who is not only his help meet but
also his spouse, his sexual partner. Here is a singular case: the
creature born from a man becomes his mistress. It is therefore
not only the story of the birth of a daughter, but also of the
tribal ancestor's incest with her.

This feature which, as far as my knowledge goes, does not
appear in the myths of other people is conspicuous. It is astonishing that it has not aroused the attention and curiosity of all
Biblical scholars and commentators. If we accept the interpretation of reversal for the essential content of the Eve myth,
we must conclude that we find traces here of an original tradition of incestuous relation between a mother and son in primordial times. In the Biblical narrative, the incest is displaced
to the relationship between father and daughter. On this detour and in the form of this displacement, a basic feature of an

original tradition has reached the surface of a much younger or more recent myth-formation.

This feature is also conspicuous because it appears in another part of the Adam story. In my book *Myth and Guilt,*[3] I showed that the original tradition of a cannibalistic crime against God-father re-emerges in myth displacement to the original sin of eating the forbidden fruit in Eden. We are confronted with similar processes in psychoanalytic practice in which repressed material, often surprisingly, reaches the surface of conscious-ness. In the history of civilizations, too, repressed impulses and ideas retain their energy and can, under certain conditions, penetrate into the realm of current experience. We know then which emotional dynamics are responsible for such very late reappearances of lost and submerged old traditions. We call that process of re-emergence the return of the repressed from the area of the unconscious.

CHAPTER XVIII

TRADITION AND THE SECRETS OF THE PAST

THIS BOOK is the third part of a trilogy whose previous volumes were published under the names *Myth and Guilt*[1] and *Mystery on the Mountain*.[2] These three works have certain features in common. They deal with unsolved problems in the prehistory of the people who created the Old Testament and they grapple with those problems in the same manner. Also, the aim of their research is the same: they try to penetrate the darkness surrounding the earliest times of Israel and the traditions of the nomadic stage from which the Hebrew tribes emerge.

In coping with those problems, an approach similar to that of the psychoanalytic exploration of individual life recommended itself. The psychoanalytic method provided the tools to enter the concealed compartment of the individual's emotional and mental life. Freud has shown us that men are not made to keep secrets. Secrets ooze out of all their pores.

The great psychologist implied, but did not explicitly declare, that nations are also unable to keep secrets and unconsciously betray them by small signs and symptoms. In using those unobserved or neglected indications as clues, my three books endeavor to discover some essential facts of the unknown life of prehistoric Israel, its scrupulously concealed and carefully guarded tribal mysteries.

The particular case presented here is of special interest because it did not simply involve digging up customs and rites from the debris of a forgotten civilization. The task was rather to explore a secret and to break a silence of three thousand years, an absolute and severe silence imposed on the Hebrew tribesmen and strictly preserved by them. It was thus necessary to overcome strong resistances against penetration of a secret, sealed with a sacred vow by all men of the tribe.

The task would be impossible if those subterranean secrets did not send descendants of their original contents to the surface, if even after a long time no messages could reach us from the recesses of prehistoric life. We have already mentioned this phenomenon of re-emergence of the concealed in the form of offspring of submerged material, of "the return of the repressed from repression."

In *Myth and Guilt,* I tried to unearth the lost Semitic tradition of a cannibalistic crime. The analysis of the Biblical myth of Adam's original sin, as well as of other myths, enabled me to reconstruct the earliest traditions of prehistoric Israel. In *Mystery on the Mountain* I attempted to trace the Biblical narrative of the Sinai revelation back to the tradition of an initiation festival of the Hebrew tribes, a secret that was subsequently closely joined with the story of the exodus from Egypt. In the present essay the myth of Eve's birth is interpreted with the help of comparison with the puberty rites of preliterate peoples. If they can be verified the three attempts would mark a step forward, however small, toward scientific mastery of the unknown prehistory of Israel.

The great significance of the secret initiation rites of the Hebrew tribes, the importance of which has not yet been recognized by archeologists and Biblical scholars, becomes apparent in these three essays. I dare to predict that a re-evaluation of those puberty and initiation rites will lead to a new interpretation of many obscure and misunderstood stories in the Old Testament and to a transformed view of ancient Hebrew religious and social life. Future scientific workers will, I venture to believe, consider my three attempts as "exploratory research."

Here is virgin territory waiting for the patient toil of pioneers. The scope of their work is almost unlimited and they may move in any direction. The situation is comparable to that of the early pioneer who looks at his large middle-western farm while he stands with his horse and plow. Turning to the horse, he shouts: "Gee-up, go where you want to go! The whole blamed thing has to be plowed."

Let us follow some furrow at random. Every story, including the Biblical one of Eve's birth, stretches deep into the past. At the opening of his mythological novel *Joseph and His Brothers,* Thomas Mann wrote: "Very deep is the well of the past. Should we not call it bottomless?" We must, at all events, probe and press into this unfathomable world of the past.

Our attention now turns to origins of the formation of the tale—the pattern from which it emerged—for telling a tale has a history. The depth we would like to penetrate should provide the answer to the question: What was the tradition before it was shaped into a story? When we encounter it in the form of a myth, it tells us about what happens in the "Dream Time," as the Australian natives call it. It tells about the vicissitudes of gods and superhuman ancestors.

The storyteller does not try to satisfy man's elementary curiosity in explaining the workings of nature. His is not to reason why. He wants to recreate and tell the divine history and the mythology of his tribe. His is a late successor of the medicine men or of the guardians who, among primitive Australian tribes, demonstrate the adventures of supreme beings and of ancestor heroes during the initiation of boys. The initiation ritual is, as A. P. Elkin has characterized it,[3] "a re-enactment of what has occurred in the past, generally to a cult hero." The storyteller has taken the place of the actor.

The original meaning of the Greek word *mythos* was a "tale uttered by the mouth in connection with a sacred ceremony." Paul Valery once declared: "Myth is the name for everything that exists, or subsists, only to the extent that speech is its cause."⁴ But was it always that?

When we try to trace back the Biblical narratives, we first find unconnected tales of creation, of primal times, of the first human couple. Those tales, originally independent of each other, were integrated into a single unit many hundreds of years after they were first told. In the process of uniting them, some artificial and secondary braces and joints were used to hold the individual segments together and to make the story coherent. We saw an example of such a procedure: the emergence of Eve is originally a continuation of Adam's biography; after the first boy was circumcised (rib operation), Yahweh leads Eve to him. Yet this Genesis account does not connect Eve's arrival with Adam's maturity and manhood, but with the preceding account of the creation—as if Eve were created from Adam's body. It is as though the narrator wished to join the concealed initiation story with the tale of creation.

But what were the earlier stories about Yahweh, the creation and the first human couple? We have no accurate information about those early phases of the Biblical sagas, but we do have comparative material from which justifiable inferences can be drawn. They were first songs and dances and pantomimes— similar to those in which Australian natives re-enact the creation and adventures of their earliest ancestors. A developed form of such presentations can be recognized in one of the native poems of Nias, an island southwest of Sumatra. This poem, accompanied by dances, is recited at the funeral of a chief. In the poem, the creation of man is described "in couplets after the style of Hebrew poetry, the second verse repeating the idea of the first in somewhat different language."⁵ We find there a description of how the supreme god, Luozaho, saw himself reflected in the clear water of the celestial spring in which he bathed. Seeing his image in the water as in a mirror, he took a handful of earth as large as an egg and out of it fashioned the figure of Sihai.

There are numerous instances of such "performed" myths reported by the anthropologists who sometimes define this form as "mythic enaction."[6] The primitive myth producers did not tell myths; they made a song and dance of them. Wherever those performances are explained, accompanied by interpretive commentary—for instance, by the older men who instruct the boys about tribal lore—the myths belong to an early, but developed state.

All indications point to the conclusion that there must have been an even earlier phase in which dance and gesture without words were the vehicles of communication. In this area we find the source not only of myths but also of the rituals from which myths evolved. As we know from comparison of those productions with presentations of the most primitive savage Australian tribes, the scarcity of words did not preclude excellent and vivid communication. One would guess that writing was a far less effective means of preserving the tribal heritage than mimetic performance and dance.

We know very little about those dramatic heralds of myth formation. We might better understand the development from prehistoric performances to early mythic traditions if Biblical archaeologists would overcome the too narrow compartmental concept of their task. Anatole France tells us in *Le Jardin d'Epicure* that his visit to a museum of natural history led him to some melancholy reflections on the nature of science. When France visited the collections, an official very complaisantly explained to him the zoolithic objects and enlightened him on various subjects. But when they arrived at the discussion of the Pliocene period and of the first traces of man, the official turned away and, in reply to France's questions, said that was not his show case. The writer then became aware of his impoliteness and understood that one must not ask a scholar about secrets of the world that are not his specialty, because he is not interested in them. ("Les savants ne sont pas curieux.")

There are, of course, exceptions to this rule in the sphere

of Biblical archaeology. It is a pleasure for me to give credit
here to a predecessor whose research, though published fifteen
years ago, has remained unnoticed. After the first draft of this
manuscript was written, I read the excellent papers Thomas
Dawn Heald had published in the London *Folklore* in 1944 and
1945. In these articles the author points out the likenesses between the earlier form of the Genesis stories of the creation and
the rites of certain Australian tribes.[7] Distinguished by origi-
nality of observation, those articles showed the common purposes and structures, as well as the essential details, of the
two phenomena and came to the conclusion that the similarities
between the early Genesis stories and the initiation of boys in the
Australian ceremonies were both descended from an ancient
common stock. In the Australian ceremonies the rites and
dramatic performances are preserved, while the Genesis stories
represent the result of later development and are survivals of
their oral interpretation.

To give some idea of the dramatic and elementary character of
those rites, a few features of the initiation of some central
Australian tribes are sketched here.[8] After the novices are
decorated on the ceremonial ground by men, women appear and
dance with the novices. Suddenly a woman (in the relationship to
the boy of a potential mother-in-law) steps forward, strips the
boy of his decorations leaving him naked, darts her head
through his legs from behind, hoists him on to her shoulders and
runs off with him. At a spot some fifty yards from the ceremonial
ground, she sits down and clasps the boy sitting in front of her
in her arms. Behind, and close to her, other women, tribal
mothers and aunts of the boy, sit down. The rest of the women
dance in front of him. After a short time, two men run up and
seizing the boy, take him back to the ceremonial ground, while
the women flee to their camp. The meaning of this rite, in which
the boys in a violent break are separated from the mother
generation and brought roughly to the society of men, is clear.

The realistic nature of those rites will be manifest when we learn that among the Ngarigo, for instance, during the six months that the novice spends in the bush, his guardian feeds him, putting the food into the mouth.[9] As Mirca Eliade points out, the inference is that the novice is regarded as a baby and hence cannot feed himself without help. In many parts of the world, the novice is compared to a newborn infant unable to use his hands or to talk.[10]

Is it fantastic to assume that the new birth of Adam from the body of a father or guardian was also thus realistically presented in an early period of the Semitic puberty initiation? The analogy of the ceremonies of Australian aborigines, the dramatic quality of their rituals and pantomimes, with the earliest traditions of the Genesis stories, makes such an assumption plausible. We remind the reader that the scenario of those enacted myths represented all that had happened in the beginning of the world —the works and adventures of gods and culture heroes. Originally a myth is not a tale; it is not "narrated," but presented in *tableaux vivants* and in songs without words.

Seen from a certain viewpoint, early myths presented and acted out in this manner can best be compared with the playing of children who tell a story in pantomime. I suspect that in the dramatic performances of the initiation, subsequently accompanied by dialogue, lies the source of the dramatic plays of antiquity.

Joseph Cambell, who recently explored the development of mythology in a brilliant article,[11] pointed out how important the play element is in the early phases of myth. Referring to R. R. Marett and J. Huizinga, the well-known historian suggests that the whole sphere of primitive culture we call mythology is a play sphere. Huizinga wrote that "in all the wild imagining of mythology, a fanciful spirit is playing between jest and earnest."[12] In fact, a certain element of "make-believe" operates in all primitive feasts. Marett declares: "The savage is a good actor who can be quite absorbed in his role, like a child at play; and also, like a child, a good spectator who can be frightened to

death by the roaring of something he knows perfectly well to be
no 'real lion.' "[13]

This character of the initiation rites explains the seriousness
of the actors, who much later were replaced by the narrators of
the myths, and their effect upon their youthful audience. The
"fanciful element," that is Huizinga's playing "between jest
and earnest," is an immanent factor of those preformations of
myths. We recognize this very spirit in the half-playful, half-
earnest reversal of the sex roles in the tradition of Eve's birth
from Adam's side.

In tracing the Biblical saga back to the home of its prehistoric sources, we are always reminded that we are transferring
and transforming primitive ways of thought into modern forms
of expression. In the sphere of the early myths, pre-logical
thinking rules, a primary thought-process in which opposites can
coexist and do not exclude each other and in which notions
turn into others as easily as fairy tale figures change their
identity. Our interpretation of the myth of Eve's birth is similar
to the translation of a "forgotten" archaic language into plain
English. It is unavoidable that such translations often fail to
convey faithfully the meaning of the original. The philosopher
Franz Rosenzweig, to whom we owe an accomplished German
translation of the Bible, once stated that there is no such thing
as good and better translations: there are only bad and less
bad ones.

Nietzsche wrote: "One's own self is well hidden from one's
own self; of all mines of treasures one's own is the last to be dug
up." This sentence is also valid for groups and people; there also
each is farthest from its own self and must go in search of it.
The only road leading to this self-knowledge and self-acknowl-
edgment is digging up the secret life of the prehistoric past. In
this sense psychoanalysis as applied to groups is the archaeology
of the soul.

CHAPTER XIX

PEEKING THROUGH CRACKS

THE TRIUMPH of archeology is not in unearthing unknown and valuable objects, but in making us feel we are in the presence of living men and women. Sir Mortimer Wheeler, a leading British archeologist, summed up the purpose of his long and fruitful work,[1] "We are not digging up things, but people." The young branch of psychoanalytic research in the service of reconstructing the prehistoric past has been compared here with archaeological work. This similarity is also apparent in the importance the explorer attributes to details, to the sequence and the structure of elements. The intensive scrutiny of the minutest fact which no one would have thought worthy of attention is common to modern archaeology and to the psychoanalytic approach. W. M. Flinders Petri, often called the founder of Palestinian archaeology, established the need for scrupulous and accurate recording of every scrap of evidence, asserting that pottery is "the essential alphabet of archaeology." He estimated that, in the six weeks during which he worked at Tell-el-Hesi near Gaza, he looked over fifty thousand or more pieces of pottery.

The observation and psychological evaluation of slips of the tongue, gestures and other neglected small symptoms in clinical psychoanalysis can properly be compared to such minute scrutiny. The analyst follows those clues like a psychological detective and his method enables him to draw most valuable inferences from that "refuse of observation."

The theory of psychoanalysis has been worked out and elaborated to an astonishing degree; a vast amount of knowledge and insight has been accumulated over the past sixty years. A systematic exploration of unconscious processes is facilitated by the long work of many analysts.

Yet the most rewarding insights into the motivation and dynamics of unconscious life still come as surprise to the psychoanalyst. This kind of spontaneous creative experience often arises from the study of material first beginning with a hunch or vague notion. The experience of surprise results from the encounter at an unexpected moment or in unexpected circumstances of some facts for which expectation has become unconscious. Surprise is essentially due to confirmation of an unrecognized, often repressed, expectation. We experienced such a surprise when the vague idea of the secret meaning of the Eve myth first emerged from material so often and for so many centuries studied by Biblical scholars and students of comparative mythology. It was as if something long forgotten had suddenly sprung up out of the middle of the familiar, as if we were confronted with a notion which had been hidden from our conscious thought, something once known but not acknowledged, some concept alien because it had become alienated.

There are crucial experiences analogous to such surprising discoveries in modern archeology comparable in their importance to Freud's findings, arising from soil that has often been cultivated. When G. Maspero, director of the Egyptian antiquities department, gave Lord Carnavon the concession for digging, he warned: "The age of discovery in the Valley of Kings is passed."[2] Every grain of sand there had been sifted and turned, or so it seemed, and further investigation seemed to be a waste of time. Yet in November 1922, Lord Carnavon and Howard Carter found the entrance to the tomb of Tutankhamen and with it a plentitude of the most valuable treasures of dynastic Egypt.

There are also moments of suspense common to the archaeologist, who digs in search of the past of people, and the analyst, whose exploration tries to penetrate the recesses of the repressed and forgotten in prehistory—moments of suspense preceding the felicity of the great findings. When Howard Carter tore down some workmen's huts in the Valley of Kings, a stone step cut into the rock was found, then another and another, until finally part of a doorway, blocked and sealed, was discovered. The seal was that of a royal necropolis. Weeks later, in the flickering light of candles, Carter distinguished shapes, shadow and colors down there. There were wondrous things. He had looked into the ante-chamber of a king's tomb. He and Lord Carnavon already knew that they had discovered something especially valuable—even before they saw Tutankhamen's coffin.

In the work of archaeologists preceding Howard Carter, there are many such cases of looking through the cracks, as in that of the American Theodore Davis who discovered the mummy and coffin of the great "heretic king" Amenophis.

We venture to compare the findings of archaeological psychoanalysis with the early discoveries of those scholars who explored the remote past of Egypt and Babylon. The trilogy whose third part is presented here tries to open the entrance into a hidden shaft which promises valuable insights into the religious and social life of the remote past. We too are trying to peer through the cracks into the depth. The question raised at this point is: does recognition of the secret initiations of Semitic tribes provide such a peephole into the early undiscovered life of the tribes who were later united as the Hebrew people? In the weak and indistinct light of the depths into which we have descended, what can be seen behind the interpretation of the Eve story?

Emerging from the mist and murk of mythological elaborations and configurations, we have been confronted with a new and surprising view: Eve's creation saga presents itself as a distorted and displaced part of the initiation ceremony, especially of the rebirth of the novice, followed by the choice of a consort. The myth of her birth no longer appears as a singular and isolated production of fantasy; the figure of Adam no longer seems the grotesque freak of a man who brings a daughter whom he marries into the world. (We are here again reminded that on this detour the repressed incest of mother and son returns in the saga in the form of a reversal.)

When we now direct the beam of our searchlight to the ground of the pit, we seem to recognize a human being. We have learned that his name is Adam—or was Adam, before his name became mud. But is he human? According to Hebrew folklore, he was superhuman. We heard that he was so tall that he filled the world, and Yahweh had to reduce him in size. We are told that in the beginning the angels worshipped him and thought there were two powers. Yahweh had to take measures to prevent his worshippers from believing that Adam was His co-worker in the Creation. The mythical figure of our first ancestor was, like the cult hero of all ancient oriental people, originally supposed to have been superhuman—a god or a demigod. He became human and, finally, all-too-human, in the pre-Biblical myth many centuries after the primal tradition was forgotten and suppressed. In the beginning, there must have been a myth in which that divine being was not only the product of God, but also his son and a god like his father. When the world was created, this son-god was already there.

Do we recognize here a melody that has been heard before, and which subsequently often returned variously elaborated? It is possible that there will be no "Second Coming" of Christ, but it is certain that a similar figure arrived many times before the appearance of Jesus of Nazareth. He had many divine predecessors in Egypt, as well as in Babylonia, Greece and Canaan.

The story of the Judaeo-Christian religion shows that there is unity, consistency and continuity in the development of the myths reaching from Adam to Christ. Christ is called the "heavenly Adam" (I Corr. XV:49) and the "last" Adam. The analogies and contrasts of the vicissitudes of the first and second Adam were extensively discussed by the church fathers and by later theologians. In spite of such long and detailed comparisons by historians and Biblical scholars, an irresistible conclusion was not, as far as I know, drawn, namely, that the original pre-Biblical Adam figure of the Semites was a god, a son-god similar to Osiris, to Adonis, Attis and finally to Jesus Christ.

The earliest traditions of the Semites, we assumed, must have known such a son-god, who was later degraded to the rank of a primal human being. This god, and son of god, was not only anthropomorphized and made into a man, but reduced to a subhuman person. A late descendant of his was then again deified, transfigured and idolized. The first Adam was originally identical with the second, a genuine "Son of Man." Jesus Christ is his "revenant"—the same figure, elevated, reinstated, restored and re-established, a second and improved edition, provided with a positive sign.[3]

Yahwism did not tolerate a son-god. The exclusive deity of Moses did not permit the existence of another god-like being besides him. The god of Mohammed called forth a holy prophet from a virgin mother, but he too "begetteth no children." The Koran says (XX): "It is not meet for God that He should have a son; God forbid! When He decreath a thing, He only saith unto it 'Be' and it is." As W. R. Smith points out,[4] the idea of divine fatherhood was in early Hebrew religion already "entirely dissociated from the physical basis of natural fatherhood. Man was created in the image of God, but he was not begotten; God-sonship is not a thing of nature, but a thing of grace." We know this was not always so: the gods of the Semites produced children in the natural way, just as the mortals do. As a matter of mythological fact, those gods were mortal. Only later was procreation replaced by creation.

In the original tradition, Adam is the son of *Adamah,* which means of earth; therefore, he was born of an earth goddess. Many commentators (Hugo Gressman, for instance) have recognized in the figure of Eve an ancient goddess, a deity of the underworld, sometimes personified by a snake. Some of the

Mediterranean deities are represented with snakes in their hands
(the Arcadian Artemis, Hecate, Persephone) or in their hair
(the Gorgon, the Erinyes). It is doubtful if Gressman's particular theory is correct, but he is certainly right in assuming
that the Biblical Eve is a late representative of an ancient
goddess.[5] In the oldest Semitic tradition, Adam, the son of the
Adamah, was the son and lover of the goddess of the Earth.
The severe cult of Yahweh banned those deities into the nether-
world or, as in the case of Eve, deprived them of their divine
character. After more than two thousand years, the figure of a
mother-goddess re-emerged. The female principle that had perhaps preceded the male gods returned in the form of the Holy
Virgin.

Are the figures of the "Great Mother," as the Phoenicians
called their goddess, and of her divine son really absent in the
prehistoric religion of the Hebrews? We feel that we can recognize their dim contours in the Biblical shapes of Eve and Adam;
or rather, in their predecessors in a lost tradition.[6]

Our searchlight has illuminated only a small space of the
secret compartment reserved for the original traditions. (We are
reminded of Portia coming home to Belmont: "The light we see
is burning in my hall; how far that little candle throws his
beams.") Helped by the immense labor of love and learning of
archeologists and Biblical scholars, we have arrived at a new
frontier of research awaiting the future work of archaeological
psychoanalysis. The age of discovery in this field will resurrect
the lost world of Semitic mythology the picture of which is still
changing. The secret initiation rites, whose significance was discussed in this book, will have their place in this new view. I hope
their importance in the formation of myth and ritual, tradition
and history, has become manifest in the trilogy that now comes
to a close in this book.

It only remains to be added that the analogy between the
initiation rites and the Semitic myths can be followed even into
the realm of myth development. One of the crucial parts of the

initiation ceremonies is the sudden and violent break which occurs between sons and mothers. An analogous evolution must have taken place in the pre-history of the Hebrew people, perhaps long before they entered the Fertile Crescent and certainly before their infiltration into Canaan. In a violent reaction against the pagan cults in which goddesses and their divine sons became lovers, the figures of the divine mothers together with their son-consorts were eliminated. In another book,[6] we traced this complete and abrupt ejection back to Moses and his introduction of the new and intolerant Yahwah cult. This religious and social revolution (continuing for a long time and often interrupted by relapses into the cult of Baal and Anath, as well as into sacred prostitution) secured the autocracy of Yahweh and forever excluded any other god. In other civilizations of the ancient Middle East, mother-goddesses remained consorts of their divine sons, were sometimes fused with figures of male gods or were restricted to certain functions reserved for them.

In descending the shaft whose entrance we discovered, the real character of the myth of Eve's creation became recognizable to us. It is not what it seemed to be to the average reader of the Genesis narrative, but is the veiled tale of Adam's rebirth in the puberty rites. Tracing the tale down to its mythological roots, we realized that Eve was the representative of an ancient mother-goddess. There is nothing mystical and mysterious in her birth, the story of which preoccupied the imaginations of so many theologians and scholars. We must finally return to the original cosmological conception as told in the first chapter of the Bible according to which God created male and female together.

Behind the mythological smoke screen the image of Eve as earth-goddess has emerged, of Mother Earth who was the womb and the tomb of all plants, animals and men. The Yahwistic narrator reminds man of this humble origin in that fateful sentence: "For dust thou art and unto dust shalt thou return."

Letting our thoughts drift from the primordial world to our own, and to this our age of reason, we might wonder at our-

selves, and at our stupid and stubborn pride. Vanity of vanities!
The white man imagines that he is made of nobler dust than the
Negro and the Gentile of more valuable earth than the Jew. The
human male animal finds reason for higher self-esteem in the
thought that he will crumble unto better dust than the female.

POSTSCRIPT

"THE GOD whose oracle is at Delphi neither speaks plainly, nor conceals, but hints," says Heraclitus. Unlike those of Apollo, the utterances of Yahweh are not obscure. The ways of the Lord may be dark but his words are not ambiguous. The disguises and distortions in the Hebrew tradition are not his work, but those of his worshippers.

The myth of Eve has been dissipated. The mystery of woman that has intrigued all men since the day of her creation remains unsolved.

How did our ancestors meet the challenge of the other sex? Looking back at the Yahwistic report of Eve's creation, the impression remains that it was conceived in a spirit of hostility to women. Our sketchy survey of the rabbinical and early Christian commentaries shows that the misogynous attitude toward Eve prevailed until the end of the Middle Ages, rarely interrupted by flickers and flashes of friendlier feeling.

Holy Scripture does not say much about how Adam felt about his help meet. Mark Twain, who found Adam's diaries, quotes the following sentences from them: "After all these years, I see that I was mistaken about Eve in the beginning. It is better to live outside the Garden with her than inside without her." Adam found it easy to be original since, as Mark Twain remarked, ". . . when he said a thing, he knew nobody had said it before." Those sentences embody, thus, the first man's well-considered opinion concerning Eve.

The last word has not yet been spoken. Everybody knows that inevitably woman has the last word.

NOTES

INTRODUCTION

1. The description relies on accounts from Irving Stone, *Clarence Darrow for the Defense*, New York, 1949, and Arthur Weinberg, *Attorney for the Damned*, New York, 1950.
2. In a letter to C. G. Jung, dated December 7, 1911, as quoted by Ernest Jones, *The Life and Work of Sigmund Freud*, Vol. II, p. 452, New York, 1955.
3. In my book, *The Search Within*, New York, 1956.

Part One: The Myth and Mystery of Eve

CHAPTER I: THE TWO STORIES

1. For instance, Salomon Goldman, *In the Beginning*, New York, 1949, p. 84.
2. Gerhard von Rade, *Das erste Buch Moses*, Göttingen, 1953, p. 34.
3. *ibid.*, p. 11.
4. See the comments on these legends in Louis Ginsberg, *Legends of the Jews*, Philadelphia, 1909, Vol. V.
5. Goldman, *op. cit.*, pp. 84-85.

CHAPTER II: THE FIRST HUMAN BEING A MAN-WOMAN?

1. James Frazer, *Folklore in the Old Testament*, New York, 1925, p. 4.
2. *ibid.*, p. 49.
3. *ibid.*, p. 1.
4. *ibid.*, p. 47.
5. von Rade, *op. cit.*, p. 45.

6. Cf. passages quoted by Ginzberg, *op. cit.*, Vol. V, p. 88.
7. *The Old Testament in the Light of the Ancient East*, London, 1911. Index s.v. Androgynous. Mirca Eliade pointed out (in *Patterns of Comparative Religion*, London, 1958, p. 423) that many primitive Australian societies hold that their primeval ancestor was a hermaphrodite. In Scandinavian mythology we also encounter the hero Tuisco who is androgynous. The Catholic missionary J. Winthuis asserts (in *Das Zweigeschlechterleben bei den Zentral-australiern und anderen Völkern*, Leipzig, 1928) that the primitives of Central Australia present the ancestor of the human being as a bisexual creature and follow the belief in a primal androgynous being in the religions of ancient Persia, Greece and Israel. Herman Nunberg (*Problems of Bisexuality As Reflected in Circumcision*, London, 1949, p. 15) refers to F. Lenormand (*Les Origenes de l'Histoire*, Paris, 1860, Vol. I, p. 51) in assuming that the prepuce represents the female part of the man and arrives at the interpretation that God circumcised Adam and made a woman out of his prepuce. In a recent paper ("A Note on the Bisexual Origin of Man," *Psychoanalysis*, Vol. 8, No. 3, Fall 1957) Rose Palm deals with the concept of the androgynous origin of man.
8. Ginzberg, *op. cit.*, Vol. V, p. 89.
9. *Talmud*, tr. Berachoth 761.
10. *Adam*, Munich, 1955.
11. An English translation by F. Friedberg-Seeley and Jean H. Barnes was published in London in 1937 under the title *Philosophy of Love*.
12. *ibid.*, p. 345.
13. "Die Biblischen Schöpfungsberichte," *Archiv. für Religionswissenschaft*, Vol. IX, p. 171, ff.
14. *Paradies und Sündenfall*, Munich, p. 241.

CHAPTER III: ADAM AND THE ANIMALS

1. R. B. 17, 4, quoted from J. Dreyfus, *Adam und Eva nach der Auffassung des Midrasch*, Strassburg, 1894, p. 19.
2. Ginzberg, *op. cit.*, Vol. V, p. 87.
3. "Adam and Eve in Babylonian Literature," *The American Journal of Semitic Languages and Literatures*, Vol. XV, No. 4 July 1899.
4. *ibid.*, p. 202.
5. Some commentators have asserted but not proved that a Baby-

lonian myth was the prototype for the Yahwistic story of Adam and Eve. (Cf. L. King, *The Babylonian Religion and Mythology,* London, 1895, p. 113; H. Zimmern, *Die Keilschriften und das Alte Testament in Religion und Sprache,* Berlin, 1903, p. 528; and P. Keil, *Zur Babel und Bibelfrage,* p. 59.) H. Gunkel, *Genesis,* 3rd edition, p. 55 and other scholars reject that hypothesis. A. Loisy called Jastrow's identification of the names of Hawwa and Ukhat *"très risqúe."* ("Les Mythes Babyloniens et la Genèse," *Revue de l'histoire et de la literature Religieuse,* VI, p. 190.)

6. *ibid.,* p. 208.
7. *Die Traumdeutung,* Gesammelte Schriften, Leipzig, 1925, Bd. II, p. 206.
8. According to Abboth Rabbi Nathan (as quoted in *Encyclopedia of Biblical Interpretation,* by Menachem M. Kasher, New York, 1953, Vol. I, p. 66.)
9. Ginzberg, *op. cit.,* Vol. V, p. 79.
10. *ibid.,* Vol. II, p. 86.

CHAPTER IV: THE RABBIS

1. Ginzberg, *op. cit.,* Vol. I, p. 66.
2. August Wunsche, *Schöpfung und Sündenfall des ersten Menschenpaares im jüdischen und moslemischen Sagenkreis,* Leipzig, 1906, p. 22.
3. Joseph Gaer, *The Lore of the Old Testament,* Boston, 1952, p. 45 ff.
4. Frazer, *op. cit.,* p. 2.
5. Some scholars assume it was Hadrian who liked to dispute with Jewish and other scholars. Rabbi Gamaliel, also known as Gamaliel of Jabneh, visited Rome twice. Cf. Menachem M. Kasher, *op. cit.,* p. 113, footnote.
6. Dreyfus, *op. cit.,* p. 21.
7. Ginzberg, *op. cit.,* Vol. I, p. 34.
8. *ibid.,* Vol. I, p. 67.
9. Kasher, *op. cit.,* p. 114.
10. Ginzberg, *op. cit.,* Vol. I, p. 67.

CHAPTER V: BONE OF CONTENTION

1. This and some other facts are quoted from Max Kemmerich, *Kultur kuriosa,* Munich, 1926, 2 Bd., p. 26 ff.

2. M. Roth, *Andreas Vesalius,* Berlin, 1892, p. 155.
3. Kasher, *op. cit.,* p. 115.
4. Erubim fol. 18a (Cf. Berachoth fol. 61a).
5. Oskar Dahnhardt, *Natursagen,* Leipzig and Berlin, 1908, Bd. I, p. 115 ff.

CHAPTER VI: THE POETS

1. Without an author's name, printed for John Bull, London, 1774.
2. The verses cannot be found in many editions of Moore's *Poetical Works* but the edition of 1826, 4th Volume, contains them.
3. In *Poems of a Jew,* Random House, New York, 1940, p. 63.
4. May 3, 1866. (Quoted in William H. Hondon, *The Hidden Lincoln,* Garden City, 1940.)

CHAPTER VII: TOO-SMOOTH SAILING

1. Cf. *Das Neue Drama,* Berlin, 1915.
2. Letter of April 26, 1927, published in *Die Neue Rundschau,* 68, 1957, I, 12:11.
3. *The Book of Genesis,* London, 1904, p. 41.
4. *ibid.,* p. 43.
5. von Rade, *op. cit.,* p. 65.
6. Published in New York and Nashville, 1952, Vol. I, p. 500.

CHAPTER VIII: THE COMMENTATORS

1. Ernest R. Trattner has tried to follow this development in his recent *Unravelling the Book of Books,* New York, 1959.
2. *Scholia On the Old Testament,* Oriental Institute Publications, Chicago, 1931, p. 23.
3. For instance in Pirkod Rabbi Eliezer, Chap. 2, T. S. (as quoted in Kasher, *op. cit.,* p. 117.)
4. Quoted by Howard W. Haggard, *Devils, Doctors and Drugs,* New York, 1929, p. 110.
5. 1780-1783, Vol. 3, new edition, 1824, Vol. II, p. 2, 158, 182, etc.
6. *Comment in Genesis,* Paris, 1895, p. 149.
7. *Die Genesis,* Freiburg, I. B., 1899.
8. "Innocence et Pèche," in *Revue Biblique,* 1897, p. 365, 368.
9. *Genesis,* 2nd edition, p. 91.
10. *Adam and Quain,* Leipzig, 1907, p. 8.
11. In *The Abingdon Bible Commentary,* Cincinnati and Chicago, 1929.

12. *Genesis, I-XI,* London, 1953, p. 67.
13. E. Gigot, *Special Introduction to the Study of the Old Testament,* New York, 1901, p. 166.
14. *Handkommentar zum Alten Testament,* Göttingen, 1910, p. 9.
15. Gunkel, *op. cit.,* p. 10.
16. *The International Critical Commentary,* Genesis, p. 68.
17. von Rade, *op. cit.,* p. 67.
18. *Schöpfung und Fall,* Munich, 1957, p. 72.
19. "The Paradise Narrative in *Genesis,*" *Journal of the Manchester University Egyptian and Oriental Society,* New York, XXII, 1936, p. 28.
20. *Probleme der biblischen Urgeschichte,* Lucerne, 1947, p. 54.

CHAPTER X: THE PSYCHOANALYTIC INTERPRETATION

1. Jones, *op. cit.,* Vol. II, pp. 452-53.
2. Leipzig and Vienna, 1919, p. 113 and 118.
3. Theodor Reik, *Myth and Guilt,* New York, 1956.
4. "And Adam was a gardener," from Shakespeare's *Henry VI,* Part II, Act IV, Scene 2.

CHAPTER XI: A NEW APPROACH IS NEEDED

1. First published in the magazine *Imago,* then edited by Sigmund Freud, 1915, and now contained in my book *The Ritual,* New York, 1919.
2. Cf. Theodor Reik, *The Search Within,* New York, 1956.
3. In German: "Tja—dafür hat die Phantasie gereicht."

PART TWO: THE SOLUTION

CHAPTER XII: THE GREAT TRIBAL MYSTERY

1. *Altersklassen und Männerbünde,* Berlin, 1902.
2. James Frazer, *The Golden Bough,* Vol. II, third edition, London, 1913, p. 278.
3. Vienna, 1918. English translation New York, 1918.
4. "The Puberty Rites of Savages," *Imago,* Bd. X, 1913, and now in Reik's *The Ritual,* New York, 1931.
5. Reik, *Mystery on the Mountain,* New York, 1959.
6. Mirca Eliade, *Birth and Rebirth,* New York, 1958.
7. A. van Gennep, *Les Rites de Passage,* Paris, 1909.
8. Eliade, *Birth and Rebirth,* p. XIII.

9. *Magic, Science and Religion,* and Other Essays, Glencoe, Illinois, 1948, p. 21.
10. Eliade, *Birth and Rebirth,* p. 6.
11. A. P. Elkin, *Aboriginal Men of High Degree,* Sidney, 1946, p. 13.
12. D. F. Thompson, "The Hero Cult, Initiation and Totemism on Cape York," *Journal of the Royal Anthropological Institute,* 1933, p. 474.
13. *The Native Tribes of South-East Australia,* London, 1940, p. 626.
14. R. G. Matthews, "The Burbung of the Wiradjuri Tribes," *Journal of the Royal Anthropological Institute,* 1896, p. 311.
15. Eliade, *Birth and Rebirth,* p. 53.
16. *ibid.,* p. 54.
17. James Frazer, *The Belief in Immortality,* London, 1913, Vol. I, p. 250.
18. James Frazer, *The Golden Bough,* London, 1913, Vol. II, p. 249.
19. Cf. Eliade *Birth and Rebirth,* pp. 28 and 31.
20. E. Anderson, *Contribution a l'ethnographie des Kuta,* Upsala, p. 213.
21. E. O. James, *Primitive Ritual and Belief,* London, 1915, pp. 16-17.
22. The article on circumcision in Hasting's *Encyclopedia of Religion and Ethics,* Vol. III, p. 679.
23. *Arabia Deserta,* Cambridge, 1887-1888, Vol. I, p. 128.
24. *The Ritual,* London, 1931, *Myth and Guilt,* New York, 1957, and *Mystery on the Mountain,* New York, 1959.

CHAPTER XIII: NEW CLUES

1. Origines, Contra Celsum, 4, 38, as quoted in Ginzberg, *op. cit.,* Vol. V, p. 89.
2. Eliade, *Birth and Rebirth,* p. xi.
3. R. G. Matthews, *op. cit.,* p. 297.
4. Eliade, *Birth and Rebirth,* pp. 90-93.
5. *ibid.,* p. 93.
6. Cf. Traugott Mann, *Der Islam einst und jetzt,* Leipzig, 1914, p. 24.
7. *Genesis I-IX,* p. 68.
8. *Universal Jewish Encyclopedia,* New York, 1941, Vol. IV., p. 198.

9. *Das Hebräische Denken im Vergleich mit dem Griechischen,* Göttingen, 1952, p. 79.
10. *Beiträge zur Orientalischen Mythologie,* Leipzig, 1904.
11. *Das Inzestmotiv in Dichtung und Sage,* Leipzig, 1912, p. 317, and *Psychoanalytische Beiträge zur Mythenforschung,* 2nd Edition, Leipzig and Vienna, 1922, p. 77.

CHAPTER XIV: ADAM'S CIRCUMCISION

1. For instance, R. Jachanaan, *Bereschitch,* p. 14.
2. *Analyse der Phobie eines fünfjährigen Knaben,* Gesammelte Schriften, Vol. VIII.
3. E. Crawley, *The Mystic Rose,* New York, 1927, Vol. II, p. 21.
4. W. Koppers, *Primitive Man and His World Picture,* London, 1952.
5. Eliade, *Birth and Rebirth,* p. 74.
6. Alfred Jeremias, *Das Alte Testament im Lichte des Alten Orients,* 2nd edition, Leipzig, 1906.
7. Eliade, *Birth and Rebirth,* pp. 92-93.
8. F. B. Jevons, *Introduction to the History of Religion,* London, 1896, p. 52.
9. *Hand-Kommentar zur Genesis,* p. 25.
10. *Urgeschichte,* Leipzig, 1883, p. 46.

CHAPTER XV: THERE'S THE RUB

1. W. S. and K. Routledge, *With a Prehistoric People,* London, 1910, p. 151.
2. James Frazer, *Balder the Beautiful,* Vol. II, pp. 249-250.
3. G. W. Harley, "Notes on the Poro in Liberia," *Papers of the Peabody Museum of American Archeology and Ethnology,* 1941, p. 15.
4. Bruno Bettelheim, *Symbolic Wounds,* Glencoe, 1945, p. 219.
5. *Male and Female,* New York, 1949.
6. The relative value of the evidence contained in ritual behavior and in myths has become the subject of many controversies. Cf. for example W. R. Smith, *Religion of the Semites,* 2nd edition, London, 1894, p. 17 ff.; D. G. Brinton, *Religions of Primitive People,* New York, 1897, chapter III, p. v; and the article on religion by Stanley A. Cook in *Encyclopedia of Religion and Ethics,* Vol. X, p. 666.

158 NOTES

CHAPTER XVI: A HOAX IN THE STONE AGE

1. Ehrenreich, *Die Mythen und Legenden der südamerikanischen Urvölker*, Leipzig, 1905, p. 46. Another instance appears in Böklen, *Adam and Quain*, p. 106.
2. Abridged edition, New York, 1927.
3. A Cape York native said that the novices are "stolen from the mother." (D. F. Thompson, *op. cit.*, p. 474.)
4. Bettelheim, *op. cit.*, p. 109.
5. See my paper, "The Puberty Rites of Savages," in *The Ritual*.
6. T. W. M. Whiting, *Becoming a Kwoma*, New Haven, 1941, pp. 90-91.
7. Curtis D. MacDouglas, *Hoaxes*, New York, 1958, p. vi.

CHAPTER XVII: ABSURDITY AND MOCKERY IN THE EVE MYTH

1. In my book *Of Love and Lust*, New York, 1941, p. 534.
2. Cf. the examples in Funk and Wagnall's *Standard Dictionary of Folklore, Mythology and Legend*, New York, 1949, Vol. I, p. 5 and p. 515.
3. New York, 1957.

CHAPTER XVIII: TRADITION AND THE SECRETS OF THE PAST

1. New York, 1956.
2. New York, 1959.
3. *Aboriginal Men of High Degree*, Sidney, 1938, p. 43.
4. Frazer, *Folklore*, p. 7.
5. Henry A. Murray, "Myth and Mythmaking," *Daedalus* (Proceedings of the American Academy of Arts and Sciences, Vol. 88, No. 2, Spring 1959), p. 214.
7. "The Earlier Form of the Genesis Stories of the Beginning," *Folklore*, Vol. LV, Sept. 1944; and "The Earlier Form of the Story of Cain's Birth," *Folklore*, Vol. LVI, March 1945; and "The Still Earlier Form of the Story of Cain's Birth," *Folklore*, Vol. LVI, Sept. 1945.
8. B. Spencer and F. J. Gillen, *The Northern Tribes of Central Australia*, London, 1904, p. 237 ff.
9. A. W. Howitt, *The Native Tribes of South East Australia*, London, 1904, p. 563.
10. Eliade, *Birth and Rebirth*, p. 15.

11. "The Historical Development of Mythology," *Daedalus,* Spring 1959.

12. J. Huizinga, *Homo Ludens,* London, 1949, p. 5.

13. *The Threshold of Religion,* New York, 1914, p. 48.

CHAPTER XIX: PEEKING THROUGH CRACKS

1. Quoted in Roland Jessup, *The Wonderful World of Archeology,* New York, 1956, p. 119.

2. C. W. Ceram, *Gods, Graves and Scholars,* New York, 1952, p. 178.

3. On the parallel between Adam and Christ compare Benjamin Murmelstein, *Adam,* Vienna, 1958.

4. *Lectures on the Religion of the Semites,* 2nd edition, London, 1894, p. 41.

5. "Mythische Reste in der Paradieserzählung, *Archiv. für Religionwissenschaft,* 1908, Vol. X, pp. 345-367.

6. The assumption that the Israelites worshipped a mother-goddess and a son-god in pre-monotheistic times was first made in my book *Der eigene und der fremde Gott,* Leipzig and Vienna, 1923, p. 33. Later, Arthur Feldman, "Freud's *Moses and Monotheism,*" and "Three Stages of Israelitish Religion," *Psychoanalytic Review,* Vol. XXXI, 1944, and Herman Nunberg, *op. cit,.* p. 78, maintained that the repressed cult of the great mother-goddess and of her son-consort was replaced by monotheism. Cf. also S. H. Hooke, *The Origins of Early Semitic Ritual,* London, 1938, and from the psychoanalytic viewpoint, Ewald Roellenbeck, *Magna Mater im Alten Testament,* Darmstadt, 1949. Harold Feldman made plausible in "A Revision of Freud's Myth," *Psychoanalysis,* Spring, 1959, No. 1, the idea that the two figures of the son-god and of the father-god were merging.

7. *Mystery on the Mountain,* New York, 1959.